FORGOTTEN PEACEKEEPERS

FORGOTTEN PEACEKEEPERS

"The Story of the United States Constabulary in Germany"

JOHN CAPONE

ISBN # 0692824308

Published by Stand Up America, USA

Bigfork, Montana

Printed in the United States of America

TABLE OF CONTENTS

ACKNOWLEDGEMENTS

This book could not have been written without the assistance of the many people who unselfishly gave of their time and talent to assist me in presenting a factual account of events as they unfolded in the early days of the American occupation in Germany. Therefore, I want to express my sincere thanks to all of them, and especially to the following:

First and foremost, to my wife Diana for her complete commitment, support and most of all her encouragement during the time I was writing this book. Her valued advice, especially her suggestions and recommendations, helped me organize my work so I could express my ideas and experiences as they actually occurred. My sincere love and appreciation, Diana, for all you have done for me and for always being there.

To the men and women who served in the United States Constabulary and wore the Circle 'C' insignia during its short existence, I am hopeful that this book will highlight your accomplishments and contribution toward the establishment of a democracy in Germany that somehow has been overlooked by history.

To W. Thomas Smith, Jr., for his expert assistance in editing the manuscript, and for his support and military knowledge that helped me tell my story.

To the team at Stand Up America Publishing, for their outstanding work and support: General Paul Vallely, CEO; Heidi Roedel, graphic artist; and Kathleen Hawkins, editor. This book could not have been put together so ably without their talent and teamwork.

To Captain Hartmut Happel, member of the General staff at the former Ordensburg—now the General Oberst Beck Kaserne, home to the Feldjäger Military Police School of the German Federal Armed Forces. Captain Happel is the author of 'The Ordensburg Sonthofen,' and generously allowed me to use his photos and information that would otherwise not have been available for this book.

To Eugen Heimhuber of Fotohause Heimhuber in Sonthofen, Germany, whose father was the official photographer for the U.S. Constabulary School, for his permission to use his photos as needed for this book.

To Stephen M. Bye, Research Assistant at the U.S. Military History Institute at Carlisle Barracks, PA, for providing me with the case files from Brigadier General Henry C. Newton's papers.

To William McKale, Museum Director at Fort Riley, Kansas, for his assistance in locating source material for research purposes. He searched for and located cartons of valuable reference materials.

To Richard W. Schneider, President of Norwich University, for providing me access to the Special Collections in their

Kreitzberg Library, and to Kelly Nolin, Special Collections Librarian, and Jack Hall, Archives Assistant, for their valuable assistance in locating and providing material used in this book.

To the members of the United States Constabulary Association who shared their stories, experiences, photos, copies of military orders, and papers that contributed greatly to this story. Some materials were used and some were not, but all contributed to the spirit of this book. My deepest thanks to:

Richard Alexander, Tom Allotta, John Ames, John Berglund, Frank Broce, Edwin Cordeiro, Chester Cox, Ray Cramer, Jim Cross, Walter Cunningham, Wayne Dixon, Ludwig Fasolino, Dick Fessenden, Nickolas Fuscsick, Milton Gaddy, Manny Goldstein, James Hill, John Holcomb, James T. Holland, George Hooker, Gene Hopkins, Ron Johnson, Clarence Klinger, Maurice Knowles, Karl Kotter, James Lantz, Ewing Larby, Lowell Larsen, Walter Laute, Phil Leveque, Charles Luce, John Medak, William Medeiros, Jim Miller, William Milton, Jesus Miranda, Rose Obenhouse, Harold Owen, Donald R. Perkins, Henry Peterson, Pete Peterson, Arthur Pippenger, Salvatore Raccuglia, Albert Reinke, Remo Sabetti, Al Sallustio, Gerald Shallberg, Gene Snowden, Ralph Stovall, George Thompson, Torben Torngren, Robert Trimble, Al Vischio, Clyde Weathers, Louis Winkelman.

Thanks to Irene Moore, Toni Schindler and Pamela Volpe for their valuable contributions and assistance.

This book is dedicated to my granddaughter
Kaitlyn Elizabeth Capone,
who inspired me to reconnect with my
Constabulary experiences.

To the fine men and women of the United States Armed Forces
throughout the world who serve as peacekeepers
in distant lands:

YOU WILL NEVER BE FORGOTTEN

FORWARD

Brig. Gen. Albin F. Irzyk, USA (Ret.)

When WWII in Europe ended, Germany was not only defeated; it was demoralized, destroyed, and devastated. The country was a shambles.

The victorious nations would jointly assume the occupation of Germany by dividing it into four Zones of Occupation: Russian, British, French, and American. There were no functioning municipal, state, national, or border police and no governments at any of those levels. Additionally, the beaten country was flooded with refugees and displaced persons from virtually every nation in Europe. Tactical units were immediately put into place to prevent utter chaos.

One of those was my 4th Armored Division, which distinguished itself by spearheading the advance of Gen. Patton's Third Army all across Europe. As the war was ending, it had been told that it would be a PERMANENT Occupation Division. Accordingly, the units of the division were quickly spread out through much of the occupation zone, which was about the size of the State of Pennsylvania. They immediately started to bring law and order to the communities, and began assisting the German people to get up off their knees and to start putting their lives back together. The units were hard at work carrying out their mission when the Division received a surprising, totally unexpected blow. It was informed that it would immediately be deactivated, and would be a Division no more. Instead, it would become the nucleus of a brand-new, unique, specialized force— so special and so unique that none like it had ever before existed in our Army. It was to be a lightly-armored, highly mobile, flexible, potent, capable, colorful force especially created for the special needs of a successful occupation of the American Zone of Germany. It would be known as THE UNITED STATES CONSTABULARY.

Its Commanding General, Maj. Gen. Ernest Harmon, was quickly selected. He would turn out to be the perfect choice to supervise an absolutely mammoth transformation. There was an immediate, unprecedented sense of urgency. Hundreds of tasks, it seemed, had to be accomplished at once.

All the tactical units had to divest themselves of the many items that had made them a fearsome power during WWII— their tanks, half-tracks, artillery, and heavy engineer and ordnance equipment. To take their place would come fast, light, mobile equipment—many jeeps, armored cars, even horses and motorcycles. Its new Tables of Organization followed no previous pattern.

Equally important was the psychological change. There had to be a completely different mindset. No longer were the individuals tactical troops—fighters, warriors. Yes, they were still soldiers. However, they would have to turn their backs on their specialties—tanker, infantryman, artilleryman—and adapt quickly to their new role: soldier/policeman, Constabulary trooper.

Then almost at once—everywhere it seemed—on every vehicle, every sign, and on the helmets and shoulders of every trooper there appeared the very striking, eye-catching yellow circle with the blue "C" crossed by the red bolt of lightning. The German populace throughout the entire Zone was instantly aware that a brand-new force had "arrived in town."

The United States Constabulary officially became operational on July 1, 1946, and quickly took a firm grip on its assigned mission. Amazingly, this was less than six months after Gen. Harmon had assumed command. By any standard of measurement, this just had to be considered (at the very least) a minor miracle.

Gen. Harmon had brought all the pieces together in a minimum amount of time, and now he would demonstrate his great qualities of leadership. He was faced with one of a commander's greatest challenges. He had organized a brand-new outfit for a particular purpose, and now he would have to man it with young, inexperienced personnel.

All the while that this fledgling outfit was developing, the highly trained, combat-proven veterans were returning home in droves. To take their places came 17- to 20-year-old kids with limited military experience and service. The arriving officers and non-commissioned were not much older, and had equally limited military experience and service.

These, together, became the backbone of the Constabulary.

They faced demanding situations that had never before existed; they were confronted with unbelievable, unprecedented, demanding challenges. They had had no preparation for their jobs; they had no field manuals to study, as there had never before been anything like this. They were given tremendous responsibilities and very little direction or supervision; they were given the freedom to use their own judgment and initiative, and to improvise when necessary. They operated far and wide, in small groups, and covered lots of ground—very often with only two in a jeep; they patrolled the border—were national, state, and municipal police; raided Displaced Persons camps; policed highways. They were confronted with every temptation known to man, and although they were just youths, they resisted and did not succumb to those pressures. They were not swashbuckling, swaggering, overbearing, chest-thumping conquerors—anything but; they met their responsibilities in a professional manner, and toward the beaten, defeated Germans they were sensitive, caring, compassionate—very human; when the Germans saw them approaching with the yellow colors, the Circle "C"—they did not run and hide or recoil in great fear. Rather, they watched with gratitude and respect.

The U.S. Constabulary by their actions brought law and order, stability, and security to the American Zone of Occupation. This enabled the Germans, with their industriousness and determination and with the assistance of American military government personnel in place, to take control of their own police and government responsibilities, bringing a sense of normalcy to the German people.

At the end of six years it was determined that the German

people had progressed so well that there was no longer a need for the U.S. Constabulary, and the force was deactivated. It would be no more.

We have here a truly great success story. During that brief period of existence, the Constabulary had accomplished its assigned mission. After WWII Germany was on its knees. It was the initial 'care and feeding' that the Constabulary gave to that defeated nation that provided the boost that enabled it to pick itself up off its knees. The Constabulary helped jumpstart Germany on its way to being the great country that it is today.

And herein lies a great irony. Because it was so successful, because it did its job so well, the U.S. Constabulary existed for only six years. Its lifespan was so brief that it has been relegated to obscurity. Today, virtually no one in America, military or civilian, is aware that such an organization once existed. Amazingly, even military historians have "passed it by."

That is why it is so refreshing and heartwarming to know that this book about the U.S. Constabulary will soon be resting on bookshelves. As mentioned, a historical gap exists, and this volume will be most valuable in filling part of that void.

This book is of particular importance to me and means much to me. As Chief of Staff of the 4th Armored Division I had a very key role in the transformation described above. I served in the U.S. Constabulary during the first year-and-a-half of its existence. That time was a most defining period during a long military career.

I welcome this book, and I am profoundly grateful to the author for the great effort required to produce this deeply-needed volume.

INTRODUCTION

FORGOTTEN PEACEKEEPERS

The Story of the United States Constabulary in Germany

Shortly after the end of World War II in Europe, the U.S. War Department instituted a plan for the American occupational zone of Germany. The plan called for the creation of a highly efficient, mobile, well-trained military police force that would assure the safety and security of the German population and also be flexible enough to accomplish the various objectives of the U.S. government in its newfound role as an occupying force.

Keep in mind, the term "occupation force" did not carry with it the negative, politically-charged connotation it does today (though the role of occupation forces was not without criticism in the media.) Occupation was just a matter of fact, as has been the case with all conquering armies since the beginning of time. In point of fact, the methods and means by which the post-war U.S. Army approached its occupation responsibilities might well be seen as a model for our ground forces in the 21st century.

The Army's approach to effective occupation in 1946 was a force known as the United States Constabulary. Conceived in the earliest days of occupation (Germany collapsed in April 1945), the Constabulary was ordered into existence with an operational date of July 1, 1946. Deactivated in 1952, it had a short existence for a military unit of its size and scope.

In part because the Constabulary had such a short lifespan and its deactivated elements were absorbed into other military units—scant attention has been paid to the unit's history, its peacekeeping mission, and its accomplishments. Few soldiers today have ever heard of the U.S. Constabulary.

Only recently—with U.S. ground forces so heavily involved in peacekeeping missions around the world—has the approach taken by the now-forgotten Constabulary been reconsidered. We will revisit the unit in this volume.

Research for the book was conducted at the U.S. Army Military History Institute at Carlisle Barracks, Pennsylvania, where I had access to the extensive files and records of Brig. Gen. Henry C. Newton (then Colonel), the assistant commandant and director of training at the U.S. Constabulary School in Sonthofen, Germany, during the period in which the school's doors were open, 1946-1948.

My research also took me to Norwich University in Vermont, where Gen. Ernest N. Harmon, commanding general of the U.S. Constabulary, served as president of the university from 1950 to 1965. The Special Collections Section of Norwich's Kreitzberg Library included the personal memoirs of Harmon, which the author found interesting albeit shocking in parts. Gen. I.D. White, who commanded the Constabulary from May 1948 until it was incorporated into the U.S. Seventh Army in 1950, was a graduate of Norwich. His material was also made available to me, and is included in this work.

Numerous letters were received—and stories shared and compiled—from Constabulary veterans, including my private papers, notes, and photographs from my own service at the Constabulary School, 1946-1947.

Before the establishment of the U.S. Constabulary was announced, stories appeared in several newspapers including the New York Herald Tribune, the New York Times, and the Washington Post, which were critical—and questioned the strategy—of the occupation and the role of U.S. soldiers in Germany. For example, on January 26, 1946, the headline on the cover of the Saturday Evening Post read, "How We Botched the German Occupation."

MAJ. GEN. ERNEST N. HARMON

On January 15, 1946, Third Army headquarters announced that Maj. Gen. Ernest N. Harmon had been named commanding general of the newly formed

General Ernest N. Harmon, Commanding General, United States Constabulary

U.S. Constabulary. Harmon, who had served as commanding general of the 1st Armored Division in Tunisia and Italy, had returned to the states following the capture of Rome. In 1944, he returned to the European Theatre to command the 2nd Armored Division. In 1946, he was awarded command of the U.S. VI Corps, which became the U.S. Constabulary.

Harmon went to work building a unique soldier-police force. The "Trooper's Handbook" was written and published, covering the basic rules-and-regs of the Constabulary trooper's duties. Col. J.H. Harwood, former Rhode Island state police commander, was tapped to assist in the development of this handbook.

Then there was the school. Under Harmon's tutelage, the school focused on both developing an elite trooper and enabling infantry, cavalry, artillery, and tank destroyer units to function cohesively as Constabulary units. The subjects taught were those essential to the operation of a mobile occupation police force. They included raid tactics, patrolling, search procedures, methods of criminal investigation, arrests, maintaining police records, German history, and politics, as well as physical conditioning and self-defense techniques. High standards of personal appearance, military courtesy, and discipline were demanded.

The 'Ordensburg': former Hitler Youth School, served as U.S. Constabulary School 1946-1948.

The decision was made to locate the Constabulary School on the site of a former Hitler Youth School (also known as "the

Ordensburg") in the town of Sonthofen, Germany.

This impressive facility had been designed and built in 1934 by Dr. Robert Ley, leader of the National Socialist Democratic Workers Party (NSDAP), to train and educate the future leaders of the Nazi Party who would lead Hitler's new Germany. Harmon and his staff selected and assembled officers who had the experience, expertise and background to become the first administrators and instructors at the school. Col. Harold G. Holt, former commanding officer of the Combat Command B 13th Armored Division, served under Harmon and was named the first "school commandant."

Harmon also designed a uniform that would distinguish Constabulary troopers as members of an elite force. The new U.S. Constabulary 'Circle C' shoulder sleeve insignia was designed by Harmon himself. The shoulder insignia had a large "Circle C" on a gold background with a red lighting bolt running through it. The

The Constabulary Insignia designed by General Harmon.

colors were those of the three primary branches of service that provided the majority of the Constabulary personnel: infantry (blue), cavalry (yellow), and artillery (red). Helmets were painted with yellow and blue stripes with the "Circle C" insignia on the front. The men were issued bright golden-yellow scarves and specially-designed boots.

The first class, 532 hand-picked officers and enlisted men from throughout the occupation zone, began their studies on March 4, 1946, less than four months before the Constabulary assumed operational responsibility. During its short existence (27 months), the school graduated over 14,000 officers and men.

On September 6, 1946, Unites States Secretary of State James F. Byrnes spoke before the United States military allied powers and German officials on the restatement of policy on Germany.[1] Byrnes said:

> "....It was never the intention of the American government to deny to the German people the right to manage their own internal affairs as soon as they were able to do so in a democratic way, with genuine respect for human rights and fundamental freedoms.

> "...It is the view of the American government that the German people, under proper safeguards, should now be given the primary responsibility for the running of their own affairs.

> "Security forces will probably have to remain in Germany for a long period. I want no misunderstanding. We will not shirk our duty. We are not withdrawing. We are staying here. As long as there is an occupation army in Germany, the American armed forces will be part of the occupation army."

According to Gary Smith, executive director of the American Academy in Berlin, this address became known as the "Speech of Hope," as it was of great importance at a time when Germans "faced disorientation and uncertainty."

CHAPTER ONE

SONTHOFEN AND THE ORDENSBURG

The Nazis were calculating when they chose the training site for the party's elite paramilitary youth wing, Hitler Jugend (Hitler Youth), the party's future leaders. The site had to be inspiring, on a commanding hilltop, somewhat mystical, and above all, remote. The heights above Sonthofen (population 4,800), then the southernmost town of Germany and some 90 miles south of Munich in the Bavarian Alps, were deemed perfect.

Sonthofen (population today 21,000) is situated between two rivers, the Ostrach and the Iller, and is surrounded by lush fields, deep forests, small lakes and rivers. It lies in the middle of the snow-capped mountains of the Allgäu range.

Overlooking Sonthofen, high on a hill at the foot of the Allgäu Mountains, stands the fabled Ordensburg with its imposing bell-tower, the 165-ft. sentinel of what appears to be a medieval fortress monastery. In the background and dominating the landscape is Mount Grünten, the "guard" of the Allgäu.

*Mount
Grünten
'Guard of the
Allgäu'*

Ironically, it was this same facility built to train Hitler Youth in 1934 that the U.S. Army chose 12 years later to train its elite occupation force.

For the most part, Sonthofen was spared the punishing Allied air raids that were carried out during the war. But on April 29, 1945, just one day before French Forces entered the town (and one day before Adolf Hitler committed suicide), Allied air forces bombed the local Catholic church and a retirement home. The Ordensburg survived.

Perhaps it was fate.

PLANNING FOR THE ORDENSBURG

Following the defeat of Nazi Germany, information began surfacing from German documents—and transcripts of the Nuremberg trials—that revealed the full extent of the various training, education, and indoctrination programs which had been engineered by the Nazis. Armed with this now-public information, historians were able to piece together what proved to have been a meticulously-planned Nazi brainwashing effort targeting the minds of German youth, and subsequently bringing that youth—and future generations of them—to the cause of National Socialism.

The Ordensburg Sonthofen was part of that effort. And the events that led to the planning and construction of the Ordensburg Sonthofen began in earnest when Hitler was appointed chancellor of Germany and immediately began to consolidate and thus solidify his power.

When Hitler became chancellor in 1933, his trusted leader and longtime party member, Dr. Robert Ley, was appointed "Leader of the German Workers Front" (Deutsche Arbeitsfront or DAF) and "Protector of the German Worker." Ley had been a member of the German Workers Front since early 1923. Two years later, he became a Territorial Political District leader, and in 1928 he was tapped by Hitler to become a delegate to the Prussian (German State) Federal State Parliament. As chancellor, Hitler granted Ley authority to coordinate organized labor.

Dr. Robert Ley, Leader, National Socialist Democratic Workers Party (NDSAP)

In April 1933, Ley ordered Ernest Rohm, leader of the Sturmabeilung Para-Military Storm Troopers (Hitler's private army, also known as the "Brown Shirts"), and Heinrich Himmler, leader of the Schutzstaffel (the infamous SS, a branch of which—the Reichssicherheitsdienst—served as Hitler's personal force of bodyguards), to occupy all trade union buildings, confiscate union funds, and place union leaders under arrest. It was part of Ley's (and Hitler's) grand strategy to control the labor unions.

In one week, the opposition was crushed. Organized labor came under the direct control of the German Workers Front, and was integrated into a single division of the National Socialist Democratic Workers Party (NSDAP), all under Ley's leadership. Collective bargaining was eliminated; wages were set by a committee of the NSDAP, and German workers lost the freedom of the labor market and any progress they had achieved in the labor movement.

Ley then introduced the "Strength Through Joy" ("Kraft Durch Freude" or KDF) program, funded by deductions from workers' wages. This program—though at its heart a means by which the Nazis could strengthen their control over labor—provided numerous leisure programs for German workers who had never before enjoyed such privileges. For the first time, workers could enjoy concerts, sporting events, cruises, skiing holidays, even travel abroad. One element of the program—the "Beauty of Work" campaign—was created as a means by which the workers themselves could improve their working conditions and therefore seemingly hold a measure of state power.

With new privileges and social standing, the German worker felt a newfound sense of empowerment. In parades and huge Party demonstrations, workers could be seen marching shoulder-to-shoulder with the rank-and-file of the German Army. This gradual implementation of new social programs, as well as the efforts of the National Socialist Democratic Workers Party to satisfy and instill pride in workers who were to be the most disadvantaged by the party's new direction, enabled Hitler to

German workers marching in support of Hitler

establish a growing measure of influence over much of the German populace.

"I know the struggle between the old guard to accept our new leaders and the new direction our party is about to begin," Ley said, addressing a conference of district political leaders of the NSDAP in 1933. "But we must begin training our new leaders, the German youth, to lead the fight for the coming Germany."

Then, in a move that came as a complete surprise to those in attendance, Ley proposed the idea of establishing a series of mobile training camps, which would be located in each Territorial Political District (GAU) across Germany. The camps would be set up and operated for the purpose of ideological and political training of German youth and party members.

One of the conference attendees was the architect Hermann Geisler, a Party member who had recently been appointed Master of Buildings in the district of Sonthofen. Geisler, who had studied architecture in Munich and was working independently until his Sonthofen appointment, was also headmaster of the NSDAP area school in the town of Blaichach. His brother, Paul, was the Nazi district leader in Munich.

In his book, "The History of the Ordensburg Sonthofen," Captain Hartmut Happel[1] relates the following series of events that took place in early 1934:

Ley authorized Geisler to begin preliminary studies and design-planning for the mobile training facilities. Geisler bitterly opposed the idea, arguing that mobile barracks were not suitable for the training of elite leaders, and that they would not adequately serve the symbolic ideals of National Socialism.

Months later at a conference of training leaders, Geisler presented Ley with a full-scale model of what he envisioned the training facilities should be. Ley was so completely overwhelmed with the beauty of the design and the functionality of the facility that he ordered Geisler to proceed with the planning.

On April 9, 1934, at a local Nazi party meeting held in the town of Immenstadt, Geisler announced that Sonthofen had been selected as the site for one of the training facilities. Three months later, Ley and Geisler—accompanied by an entourage of townspeople, district leaders, party officials, and Hitler Youth groups—toured the Sonthofen site. Geisler explained the intended use of the facilities, their functions and relationship to one another. At the conclusion of the visit, Ley ordered Geisler to proceed immediately with the construction.

CHAPTER TWO
START OF CONSTRUCTION

O n October 4, 1934, work began on the stretch of road that would lead from the main entrance of the future training facility—known as "Reich Training Burg III" (or the "Burg")—to the main street in Sonthofen, Markstrasse. Using only picks, shovels, wheelbarrows, and oxcarts, workers cut into the side of the hill to build the road.

As Captain Happel explained in

Construction of road from Ordensburg to Town of Sonthofen

his book, the actual start of building construction took place a few months later based on the original plans to build a political training center for up to 400 students and a kommandant's quarters. As further noted in papers from the collection of Col. Henry C. Newton[1], upon the completion of the first phase Dr. Ley was so pleased with the completed 'A' building that he ordered further buildings to be constructed capable of housing and having classroom space for 2,000 students.

This would be accomplished in three construction periods:

1. B and C building (Allen Hall), tower, dispensary, academic headquarters wing, gymnasium, and kitchen: Spring 1936-spring 1939. During this period, the construction of the athletic field was also started.

2. Building 31-1 (Bandholtz Hall), Building 32-I (Rivers Hall, swimming pool, gymnasium II (the last two facilities were not completed)): Fall 1937-summer 1939.

3. Building 31-11 (civilian barracks and laundry), Building 32-11 (engineer supply building and utilities shops), incomplete: Winter 1938/39-summer 1941.

Work continued until the summer of 1941 when, because of the war effort, construction was halted.

A journal of the construction of the Ordensburg is presented in the following notes from the Henry C. Newton Papers at the U.S. Army Military History Institute ('USAMHI') at Carlisle Barracks, Pennsylvania: [During my research of the Henry C. Newton Papers at USAMHI Carlisle Barracks, the following fact sheet was found in Col. Newton's papers. It was without notation as to specific source or author, but provides an interesting chronicle of the construction.]

"Approximately 2800 workers were contracted or employed for the construction of the Burg. Included were about 1500 contract laborers from several construction firms, namely:

F.X. Amann—Lammer, Sonthofen—contractor

Josef Hebel, Memmingen—contractor (general construction)

Carl Deiring, Kempten—contractor (heating)

AllGauer Kraftwerke, Sonthofen, power company (electr.)

Fritz Herz, Sonthofen—masonry

Rudolf, Simmerberg (Lindau)—masonry

In addition to contractors, hired labor was employed: approximately 50 Austrian mason experts from Tyrol-Vorarlberg and 100 masons from the Bavarian Forests, to cover the shortage on masons; common labor was recruited mainly from Austria (after 1938), especially Vienna, but also from any part of Southern Germany, bringing the total of common laborers up to about 700. Foreign laborers, almost exclusively coming from Italy, were hired to cover the manpower shortage in Germany after the war had started. About 400 Italian masons worked on the Burg project from 1939-1941. Most of them quit after Italy declared war.

Construction material for the Burg was obtained mainly

from the vicinity of Sonthofen, the rock "Grüntensandstone" (which had an estimated durability of 500 years) was taken from Mount Grünten (Kranzegg and Burgberg quarries) and the timber from the forests surrounding Sonthofen.

The builder of the Burg (later to be called the 'Ordensburg Sonthofen') was the Deutsche Arbeitsfront (DAF) with its chief, Dr. Robert Ley. The construction costs were paid with the collected monthly fees of all German laborers, compulsory members of the DAF, and was estimated to be twenty six million dollars."

According to Happel, in October 1935, Ley delivered a speech marking the completion of the framework for the facility. In that speech—and from that point on—the building known as the "Reich Training Burg" was referred to as "The Ordensburg."

Dedication of the Bell Tower

CHAPTER THREE

ORDENSBURG AND THE KNIGHTS OF THE TEUTONIC ORDER

D r. Ley's announcement that the Sonthofen facility would be called the "Ordensburg" was startling, significant, and deliberate: In fact, for Ley to select the name "Ordensburg" and apply it to a school that would educate and train future German leaders was part of the grand mind-shaping process.

Ordensburgs were medieval fortresses built for and inhabited by the German Order of Teutonic Knights. The fortresses were built in hostile territories east of the empire, and used by the warrior monks as bases from which they could launch operations and defend against non-Christian

Ordensburg Marienburg in Marbork, Poland

enemies. The fortresses were also used as centers to train new recruits.

In the year 1190 (during the third crusade), a German Order of brothers, monks and priests was founded to provide spiritual and medical care to German crusaders in the Holy Land. A few years later, the Order was recognized by Pope Celestine III, and it became known as the Knights of the Teutonic Order.

In 1198, a change was made to include a military branch which would actively defend Christianity. The Teutonic Knights then received Papal orders to fully seize and hold Jerusalem, and defend it against Islamic expansion. At the conclusion of the

Teutonic Knights during the Third Crusade

crusades, the knights would then be ordered into action against the Muslims in Spain.

From 1231-1288—and at the request of Pope Gregory IX— the Order conquered the Baltic coast from Danzig to modern-day Estonia, converting people to Christianity and opening up Eastern Europe to mass German colonization. Settlers founded many towns and cities in these newly conquered lands, and the settled regions were organized in a military fashion with a system of impressive fortresses called "Ordensburgs."

This system of forts played an important role in the West's expansion and defense of conquered areas in the East. It was also key throughout the period as a means of providing security to tens of thousands of civilian men, women, and children who frequently took refuge inside the walls of the mighty structures during the Mongolian invasion of Europe: Time and again the Mongol horsemen were baffled by and stopped at the gates of the imposing and seemingly impenetrable Ordensburg castles.

The symbol of this German Order was the famous iron-black cross, symbolic to this day in the form of the "iron cross," which is emblazoned on all German military vehicles and aircraft. The German Order of priests, brothers, and nuns still exists throughout Germany and

Cross of the Teutonic Order

Austria today, providing a sense of physical and spiritual healing in the name of Christianity.[1]

The National Socialist Democratic Workers Party originally planned to build three Ordensburgs in early 1934. Groundbreaking took place for the first one in Vogelsgang, near the Belgian border, and construction of that facility was completed in a record time of 24 months. The "Vogelsgang" Ordensburg was built to accommodate 1,000 students. Many officials from the loftiest ranks of the Nazi party were educated there.

Party members desiring a career in the administration could pursue a four-year course in the philosophy of the new German Order. Only the brightest and most gifted youth were chosen to attend. Students had to be between 23-30 years of age. They had

Dr. Robert Ley at the Hitler Youth School; to his right, Architect Hermann Geisler and School Commandant Bauer

to belong to the Nazi party, the Hitler Youth, a work service, the S.A. or the SS. They also had to be in excellent physical condition. Students were officially called "Ordensjunkers." The faculty was hand-picked and largely comprised of SS personnel.

In a formal ceremony in 1936, Dr. Ley presented Hitler with the first of the three Ordensburgs. In his acceptance speech, Hitler emphasized the need to ensure that all guidance and education of students was to be both excellent and equally administered across Germany and throughout the National Socialistic education system.

In March 1937, the initial class completed its training and education at Vogelsgang, and from those graduates were drawn the future teachers for the Ordensburg in Sonthofen, and for the Hitler Youth Schools throughout Germany.

In his publication, "We All Help the Leader,"[2] Ley referred to his speech in the winter of 1933 at the Conference of Political

Leaders, when he first proposed the idea of establishing training facilities for the education and training of future German leaders. He stated:

"I knew the system had many flaws and it would be easy to make errors. We had no model to follow; teachers were distrustful of the seizure of power by the National Socialist Democratic Workers Party. Individual schools were strongly different from each other, subjects and curricula differed from school to school. I knew that the training at the outset was extremely unsatisfactory. Only on the basis of practice and experimentation we learned to accomplish the selection and education for the new generation of leaders."

Ley added:

"In 1933 I began planning in silence and without wavering for the construction of three Ordensburgs: Krosinsee, Vogelsgang and Sonthofen, which would become the foundation of the National Socialist Educational System. The castles had to embody the beauty and joy of life which National Socialism breathes. I did not want to use old castles because I am convinced that what we preach and teach in this new world view of Adolf Hitler cannot be taught in old dusty buildings. If I were to be asked today did I realize that my decision then would become the model for the National Socialist Educational System I would have to answer no."

CHAPTER FOUR

THE DREAM FAILS

The Nazi dream of the training and education of young men in the Ordensburgs—and preparing them for key positions in the Nazi party—was never realized. The plan, though considered an important foundation for Hitler's Reich, had to take a backseat (temporarily, it was hoped) when the nation began its massive mobilization for war and began accumulating a huge war debt. Then there was the war and the necessity of rushing all national assets toward that end. Thus the ambitious Ordensburg in Sonthofen was abandoned.

On the suggestion in 1937 of the two Reichsleiters (German leaders), Dr. Ley (NSDAP leader) and Baldur Von Schirach (Hitler Youth leader), plans were made to transform the Sonthofen facility into a Hitler Youth School.

Students were selected by Party leaders: It was not the parents' choice if or where the child would attend school. All Germans were instead "guided" by the principle, "State first, individual second." Hitler placed great importance on the German youth and on their responsibility for the future of the country.

On January 15, 1937, Hitler signed an authorization for the use of his name on the preparatory schools of the National Socialist Democratic Workers Party, to be called "Die Adolf Hitler Schule." Shortly after the Sonthofen facility was designated a Hitler Youth school, Germany began mobilizing for war, and students from the other Hitler Youth schools throughout Germany and Austria were brought to Sonthofen as a place were they could attend to their studies in relative safety.

The youth movement began to develop rapidly. Because of the camaraderie and the activities available to them, most of the boys found the programs exciting and somewhat adventurous.

Hitler Youth School Students

Beyond the classroom, the youth belonged to organizations that trained them in military skills with an emphasis on tough physical training. Each year, the boys attended camps where they learned to read maps, and they participated in paramilitary training exercises and competitive sports. Most of all, they were infused with a sense of discipline, sacrifice, loyalty, and obedience.

Most students had performance books in which marks were recorded for the various skills and athletics in which they were involved. Those students with the best records were sent to special schools to begin training as future leaders, and they were taught by the best teachers (those who had received specialized training in the instruction of superiorly performing youth). Boys from the Hitler Youth schools were given six years of training before going on to one of the universities, the armed forces, or public service. The youth schools quickly became the elite schools of National Socialism.

The capacity of the student body at Sonthofen was 2,000. Regular classes were held from summer 1938 through spring 1945. Classes provided the standard high school education plus special instruction in Nazi ideology and history, ethnology, geopolitics, political economics, and political science, among others. There were also classes in carpentry, blacksmithing, and masonry. And of course intensive physical training was a key component of Hitler Youth education.

In 1946—while a young U.S. soldier and a member of the teaching staff at the Constabulary School in Sonthofen—this author obtained a copy of the official publication "Die Adolf Hitler Schule" from a German civilian. It was prepared by the National Socialist Democratic Workers Party, and outlined the purposes and goals of the school as well as the goals which students were expected to attain. The publication was subsequently translated for the United States Constabulary School Commandant by Gerhard Kirchner, a certified interpreter, also in 1946. It provides fascinating insight into the overall plan for Germany and the specific plan to prepare future leaders.

The following is the official translation of the pamphlet entitled, "'Die Adolf Hitler Schule': The Adolf Hitler School in the year 1941 Ordinance." [1]

On a report made by the Reich's organizer of the NSDAP and the Leader of the Youth of the German Reich I herewith authorize that the new schools to be created on behalf of and for National Socialists and which are, at the same time, to be the preparatory schools for the National Socialistic Ordensburgen, bear my name.

Berlin, 15th January 1937
Signed, Adolf Hitler

[Note by translator: Ordensburgen were called in centuries gone by the castles of a religious fraternity or order.]

The Adolf Hitler School
The meaning and object of the Adolf Hitler Schools

By their name, which they proudly carry, the Adolf Hitler Schools are lifted above the large number of other German schools. In them is expressed most clearly and most distinctly the revolutionary development through which education, too, has to pass in the new State.

These schools have been established in 1937 by the two Reichsleiter Dr. Robert Ley and Baldur von Schirach in collaboration. They are being led by the Hitler Youth whose principles of education are realized here. Their teaching material, method of teaching, and the body of teachers are settled upon by the Reich's Organisator and the Reich's

Leader for the Education of the German Youths of the National Socialistic German Workmen's Party (NSDAP) on uniform lines for the whole Reich.

The leading idea underlying their establishment was the recognition of the necessity to gradually form a body of political leaders capable at one time to take over and carry on the work begun by the Führer and his faithful followers. Germany has never yet been vanquished by its enemies through sheer force of arms. It has only failed in the decisive moments for lack of a strong, uniform political leadership.

The Road of the Adolf Hitler Scholar

It goes without saying that the old, worn out roads cannot be used. New tasks demand new methods; thus the Adolf Hitler Schools differ widely on many points from the other high schools of the German Reich. Even the selection is decisive. Of course, no political leader can be brought forth by mere school training. In the end, a school can only develop, guide, and form the inherent natural gifts and talent of youth. Thence it follows that a careful selection has to be carried thro' among the mass of the people in order to find out those who in future are to be the decisive factor for the fate and the road of Germany.

Whereas, in general, the wish of the parents is decisive when choosing a higher school, in our case the decision has to be taken by the NSDAP as executive organ of the nation, as it is not a case of deciding on the future of an individual but of the rising generation of political leaders of the nation.

You are not going to the Adolf Hitler School; you are called there. The Party leaders, in collaboration with the competent Hitler Youth leaders, select from among all German youths of 12 years the most natural, the healthiest,

Hitler Youth Student Body School Formation

bravest, and most capable. It does not matter at all then from what surroundings the pupil comes, whether his father is a working man or first director, whether up till then he has attended a higher school or not. He must be able to accomplish more than the others; he must embody larger possibilities of development!

Thus, youths from all parts of the Reich, from all walks of life, will stand side by side and work in common to achieve the aim set them. They will stay at the school for six years—from their 12th to their 18th year of life—and during this time the NSDAP (Party) will undertake to look after their mental and physical welfare. The scholars will have free living quarters (lodging), free food, free clothing, free traveling, free medical treatment, all the books and teaching material they need, even a monthly pocket money, the amount of which depends on what school class the boy is in. Allowances by the parents are considered undesirable during that time in the interest of unity of education. But there is a possibility to assist and further the work of the school by voluntary donations and contributions for the foundation of the Adolf Hitler Schools.

There is no "ploughing," (failure to pass at exam) nor "promotion" at the Adolf Hitler School. The student has to prove his worth continually anew as to his readiness to tackle his task, carriage, and performance, and he'd have to leave school should he not come up to the demands required of him as to character and mental and physical fitness. After six years' successful work he obtains his

Dr. Ley reviewing student application

certificate of maturity issued by the School Board after due consideration of National Socialistic principles. Decisive in judging a boy's worth is not an examination, the result of which depends on many fortuitousnesses, but the question whether he has proved himself able during his six years' membership at the Adolf Hitler School and in as far as his attitude and his capability up till then show the likelihood of his becoming a capable political leader.

With his certificate in hand any career is open to the boy. As it is their special task to serve as eliminating schools for the "Ordensburgen," the Adolf Hitler Schools will lay special stress on the boys, in their majority, turning towards the further cultivation of the rising generation of party leaders. Youths wishing to seize the career of leader of the Hitler Youth receive their further training at the Academy for Youth's Leadership; the others can follow any calling according to inclination. They may decide on a career of handicraft or commerce, just as well as on an academic, artistic, or military career. But whichever calling he may exercise he has to feel and act as political leader.

Later on, each Gau is to have its own school. Their establishment will, in each case, correspond to the purpose and be on very generous lines. The Adolf Hitler Scholars are not to grow up amid surroundings exhaling the putrid odor of past times; they shall grow up amid light, sunshine, and fresh air; they are not to live in narrow chambers but in roomy and gaily furnished rooms; they are not to study in suffocating studies but in light floodlighted rooms; they are not to go for physical training and sport somewhere in a courtyard between stone walls but on sports grounds laid out on modern lines incorporating latest developments. The rooms in which the boys are to live shall show the same simplicity and clarity in architectural planning and inside decoration characteristic of the whole education at this school. This applies especially to the building materials, which are to show immaculate handicraft in being applied. In those parts of the Gau most favored by nature these schools are to be erected for the purpose that the boys see and live anew every day the beauties of their native country.

At present, 10 schools are intended to be built. Their foundation stones have been laid and the work of building some has already started.

They are:

1.   Tilsit
2.   Francfort-on-Oder
3.   Waldbrol
4.   Koblenz
5.   Plauen
6.   Weimar
7.   Hesselberg
8.   Chiensee
9.   Heilgendamm
10.   Landstuhl.

Until the time these buildings are ready the schools will be preliminarily housed in the Ordensburgen of the Party, or other suitable buildings.

The Work of Education

The tutors are selected from among the mass of the German body of teachers on the same principles as the boys are chosen. They are tutors as well as leaders of the youth. They have to be models in every respect—for character,

Applicant before student review board

in body and in mind—to the boys entrusted to their care. Without exception, they are young, active men with a past in political activity, a synthesis of men able to lead a Hitler Youth unit as well as efficient teachers in a lifelike and scientific way on special subjects. They are selected from among the corps of leaders of the Hitler Youth or the Party but must have proved their ability in special science.

In future, the rising generation of tutors will come from the ranks of specially selected Hitler Youth leaders prepared for their future vocation in the seminary of the Adolf Hitler School and through special training on High Schools and Institutes. The training of these prospective tutors is carried out in the spheres of science, sports, and politics.

All the tutors are leaders of the NSDAP as a main function. They are joined up in a corps of tutors and belong to the corps of leaders of the Hitler Youth. Together with the boys they form a close community of life. They are not only their superiors but also their comrades. Between them and the pupils of the Adolf Hitler Schools exists a close relation of confidence underlined informally by the use of "thou" and "thee" common in the Hitler Youth.

Certain rigid forms and regulations are necessary in a large community for the sake of the existence of this very community. They are also applied for the Adolf Hitler Schools but here they never become stiff and monopattern-like, which would compress the personality of the pupil. For this reason and as far as possible the principle of self-leadership is being applied. The boys are introduced and have

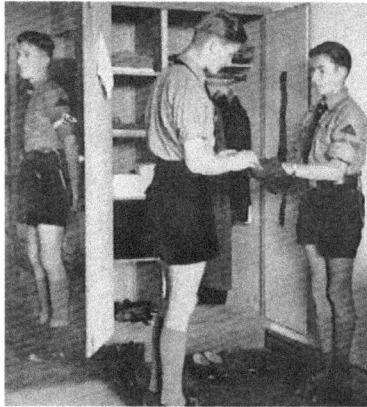

Room inspection at the Hitler Youth School

to act as leader of a small detachment, headboy of the room, leaders of working groups, team-leaders in sports, etc. Over and above that the methods of education at the Adolf Hitler Schools are synchronized in such a way that the boys not only learn to carry out given orders but that each one of them out of sheer self-discipline, responsibility, sense of honor—in short out of an inner impulse—gives to himself the laws governing his actions.

The School Work

The form of the curriculum contributes to this purpose. It differs considerably and in many respects from the standard of the other schools contingent on its particular duty to train the coming generation of political leaders. All spheres of education are envisaged from the National Socialistic point of view and assessed accordingly, raising to the foreground those of them which prove essential for the future political application in life. Physical, mental, and artistic training will have an equal share. To keep the youths in good health and further their physical training, bodily exercises of all kinds will be largely cultivated besides service in the Hitler Youth movement, putting in front sporting contests and performances, be they heavy gymnastics of the boxing-ring, sport on the lawn or the cinder-path, in the water, skiing or gliding, as pre-eminent in forming willpower and fitness to give and take.

In the sphere of mental education, ethnology and biology are considered cornerstones. Ethnology or folklore is to comprehend all provinces dealing with the taking shape and the cultural goods of German life, including German history, geography, and religious science, seen from a new point of view and formed up to a uniform whole. The branch "Look into the distance"—affiliated to Folklore—will, in particular, serve for the training in political understanding. Biology, finally, will provide the mental equipment to understand ethnology, the basis of the National Socialistic creed.

The future political leader also needs a thorough knowledge of other peoples. This he acquires when learning foreign languages, quite apart from a stay in foreign countries provided for each Adolf Hitler Scholar. Two obligatory foreign languages are included in the curriculum, with a third language for adepts at their choice.

The subjects in natural science—physics, chemistry, and mathematics—serve to widen the outlook and to further the knowledge of coherence in nature. Special value is attached to practical activity.

As for the training in liberal arts (arts education, music, and training in musical instruments) the creative forces of the youths are to be encouraged. Handicraft is to be included under this heading which, over and above its proper purpose, is of great importance in wakening in the boys—through their own hands' work—respect for the manual worker and a true understanding and appreciation of his work.

From their fourth school year onward the boys have the opportunity to perform more in the spheres for which they are particularly suited than is generally expected, be it that they take additional training in a foreign language of their own choice or turn to the natural sciences, music, artistic training, or handicraft to an increased measure.

But one thing is essential above everything else: the instructing teacher is, at the same time, educator of the boys, and in this way he can instill life and intuitiveness into his lessons. Lessons and Hitler Youth service do not clash but form a single unit. Teaching is part of the service.

The Parental Home and the Adolf Hitler Schools

The parental home forms part and parcel of the plan of education.

True, the boys must part from the parent for many weeks, but for all that the connection is not severed. On the contrary, as far as the school is concerned this link is rendered as close as possible in order to have those values imparted to the boys which only become effective in family life. Three times a year, at Christmas, at Easter, and during the great vacations the boys go home and live then together with their parents. They, on their side, have the possibility to become acquainted thro' personal contact with work and life at the school. Moreover, the boys are kept to write home regularly and the tutors, too, are keeping up a regular correspondence with their parents. During vacation they visit them and in personal discussions all the questions interesting the parents are touched upon. All this means that when the boys are called up to the Adolf Hitler School it does not mean a complete separation from the parental home.

It is true, various rights and duties pass over to the school, especially the care for their bodily well-being exercised by the doctors of the Adolf Hitler Schools. Not only are the boys examined at regular intervals, but they are under constant observation by a companionate collaboration of doctor and tutor. They are insured against sickness and accidents which extends to the vacation time spent with their parents at home. If a boy falls ill he is taken to the dispensary of the Adolf Hitler School, which is exceedingly well-equipped and where—besides the doctor—trained ambulance personnel and nurses are at his disposal. Only in serious cases or when treatment by certain specialists is considered necessary will he be brought to a public infirmary.

It goes without saying that, in such a case, the parents are notified of it, just the same as they are being kept posted about the deportment and the performances of their boys.

Life at the Adolf Hitler Schools

Four years full of events and work have, in the meantime, passed since the Adolf Hitler Schools have been built up. The beginning saw the first annual set or "form" at the Ordensburg Krussinsee [sic] up to the summer vacation. Here, the foundation was laid for the new and peculiar system of education, now become visible to all.

In the fall of 1937, the School moved to the Ordensburg Sonthofen in Allgäu which, since then, has taken in all the 10 schools into its large-sized buildings. Thus, the Burg forms the outer, all-embracing frame for the purposeful, unique work of education which, like the Burg itself, has become expressive of the creative power of National Socialism.

The boys and their tutors experience the nation's festive days always in common with the Burg community, which extends from the Kommandant down to the last charwoman and includes them all in the great tasks set to the School.

Everyday life, however, is multiform and varied. The major part of the day is spent by the boys at instruction which, in a novel form, sees boys and tutors at serious work in close working cooperation according to the principles of our creed.

Gymnastics and sport occupy the space due to them beside science and art. In winter, skiing will be the ideal activity on this important branch of education, along with indoor training. Health and naturalness in all walks of life are the springs of strength which help to fulfill the increased physical and scholastic demands of the Adolf Hitler School.

But over and above the school this education tries to make the boys members of the general life of the community, even tho' this appears to be only partly possible within such a school community which is, at the same time, a life community. The boys are distributed among units of the Hitler Youth outside the Adolf Hitler School, and there they share in Hitler Youth service. During the vacation, the Adolf Hitler Scholars are to prove their worth serving the community by work at the factories and gathering the crops and to gain an understanding for the tasks put to the German nation in life.

Notwithstanding this abundant and many-sided service enough spare time remains for each member necessary to make, by degrees, a leader out of one who has been led and a personality responsible unto his self.

Even during working hours the boy works on his own and not in community with his mates. Special importance is attached to the way in which his spare time is occupied, all this within the framework of education. The arts part of his training intentionally leads up to this sphere of spare time occupation. Singing, the playing of musical instruments, drawing, painting, woodcarving, wood and metal working, amateur theatricals, and festive hours serve this fair task.

Every visitor and critical observer may recognize the result of such a comprehensive service in the attitude characteristic of the Adolf Hitler Scholar. He may be justly proud to fight and work in the foremost front for a great end in a great time.

Regulations Concerning the Selection of Pupils for the Adolf Hitler School

Selection is carried through by the Party and the Hitler Youth in common. Notification by the parents is inadmissible. The boys are called to the Adolf Hitler School.

The boys are presented to the competent party officials within a comprehensive procedure of selection providing for special selective courses in summer camps, preliminary and final selective courses held under the leadership of the Hitler Youth. At the conclusion of this thoro' trial of fitness the Gauleiter calls the boys selected to the Adolf Hitler School.

Only the best and most efficient lads of the German people come into question who complete their twelfth year of life in the course of the calendar year of admittance.

The conditions for admittance are:

1. A perfect state of health

2. An unimpeachable character

3. Distinguished conduct in the German Young Volk, qualities as a leader

4. Proficiency in sports (minimum number of points during the Reich's sporting competition: 100 points. If at all possible the boys shall possess the Reich's certificate for swimming; country units may enter non-swimmers.)

5. Efficiency at the school

6. Uncontestable traceability of ancestry (complete and without a gap back to 1.1.1800. Children born out of wedlock are put on a par with legitimate children if these conditions are fulfilled.)

7. Proof of healthiness of stock and prolificness of kin

8. Activeness of the parents in the national community (Party membership of the parents is not absolutely necessary. However, should a selection have to be made among a number of youths of equal worth the sons of meritorious Party members are to have preference.)

Regulations Concerning the Distribution of Duties and Rights

1. For the duration of their scholastic education the Adolf Hitler School undertakes to bear the costs for lodgings, maintenance, clothing, books, school implements, trips and entertainments of the Adolf Hitler Scholars.

Over and above that the school pays to them a monthly pocket money the amount of which is gradationed according to semesters. Allowances by the parents are undesirable

The maintenance during vacation which the boys spend at home has to be undertaken by the parents.

In cases of damage or loss caused by the Adolf Hitler Scholars thro' their own fault the boys are liable to make good for up to the amount of their pocket money and should this prove inadequate the parents will become liable.

2. The Adolf Hitler School looks after the welfare of the

Hitler Youth School students marching through Sonthofen

boys entrusted to its care. This will be attended to by the school's doctor's roll-calls at regular intervals. Should a pupil fall ill he is sent to the dispensary of the Adolf Hitler School. Should treatment at the dispensary prove impossible and should, under certain circumstances, treatment by certain specialists become necessary, the decision on it will rest with the school's doctor. This also applies in case of a patient having to be sent to a public hospital or infirmary. The right of permission for an operation rests, on principle, with the parents. In cases where an operation may not prove to be of immediate necessity their consent will be asked for beforehand. In urgent cases where there is immediate danger for the life or the well-being of the boy the competent school leader may give the permission to operate. The parents are informed at once, in such a case, of the steps that had to be taken.

3. The Adolf Hitler School undertakes liability for its scholars and enters into an insurance contract against accidents and sickness. This insurance extends to the vacation, which the boys spend at their parents' home.

4. In case of Adolf Hitler Scholars whose parents live abroad the competent tutor takes upon himself the guardianship in agreement with the Organization for Foreign Countries of the NSDAP.

5. Education at the Adolf Hitler School extends over six years. The scholar has to prove his worth anew every year, however. In case of unfitness a premature discharge may take place. In this case, the parents have to take upon themselves, at once, the burden of looking after their boy for maintenance. No claim on the school may be lodged. After consulting the parents the school will, however, in agreement with the parents, look for an ulterior and suitable education of their boy at another school or in a profession, in case he does no longer come up to their special standard.

In case of moral unfitness or where false statements were made previously the Adolf Hitler School may be excluded at any time. A wish by the parents for discharge of their boy can only be granted in exceptional proved cases. Discharges take place on proposal of the tutor by the Kommandant of the Adolf Hitler School after he has previously informed the competent Gauleiter.

In all these cases the parents have the possibility to turn to the competent Gau Personnel Office as the proper office of the Gauleiter for these cases for advice and information concerning the future process of formation of their boy.

6. No legal claims against the School may be lodged except by means of Party proceedings.

Letters From Parents of Adolf Hitler Scholars

"16th February 1938
Dear Sir,

"Ulrich's birthday will be on February 25th. I have a small request to make to you for that day: I should like you to light up for him our old birthday-wreath. It has accompanied our four boys faithfully from their infancy thro' all their birthdays up to their fourteenth year, hence its somewhat dilapidated condition. Ulrich is our last boy for whom to use it and I consider there could be no better use made of it than if you were to keep it at your school and incorporate it into the first scholastic year of the Adolf Hitler School for use on the birthday table as occasion arises. As long as Ulrich is attending your school we are prepared to spend the necessary candles for this purpose.

"I was very sorry I was unable to be present at the laying of the foundation-stone in Potsdam but I had to go to Dresden on the same day. Naturally, I should have loved to talk with you about Ulrich. Many thanks for your comprehensive circular letter of January but such a letter must always fall somewhat short as its tenor must be on general lines.

"You know perhaps what it cost me to give away Ulrich just because he is our youngest boy and because his character comes up closest to my own.

"Notwithstanding his absolute youthfulness or boyishness he is very susceptible to all influences, full of sensitiveness, sensitive in sizing up the world and human beings round him. His devotion to animals exceeds the general standard. At Christmas time, for instance, his first action on coming home was to go straight to his cupboard, take the birds' food and fill up all the feeding tables. He wants me to keep him closely posted about the doings of all the animals. I knew full well from the very beginning that his early departure would hasten his growing up which naturally sets in with each child in these years. And as I consider prejudicial all excess in development I was doubly mindful. I disliked especially the restlessness of the summer semester and the many changes of residence, which the boys went thro'.

"Whereas the traces of this were clearly to be seen in Ulrich during summer there were no further traces of it at Christmas time. It seems that nature had found its own way to seclude itself internally from its outer surroundings and quietly went on its own way. So, in that respect, I have overcome all my qualms. The boy, whether here or there, will naturally develop in the same way.

"Something quite different is the common mode of living specially set up for the boys. It has done Ulrich so much good that my husband and I have seriously considered the advisability to send up our third boy to a boarding school for the last four school years he has still to do. In this respect the home of the parents is always second best only. With the best of intentions we can never attain this rigid discipline. We must still wait and see how and what the effects will be of mental training.

"I wish to seize this occasion to thank you personally most cordially for all the trouble and all the devotion you bestow on him now that you have so much to do with him. I gather from what Ulrich tells us that in many respects you continue to lead him in just the same way in which we started it at home. I shall let you know after the Easter vacations whether Uli came back to me as the same boy as which he went away at Christmas or whether I shall have been startled by anything which ought to be attended to.

"If you like, give my love to the boy. His birthday parcel proper he naturally will still get himself. This is a forerunner.

"With kindest regards and Heil Hitler! Yours ..."

"13th May 1939
Dear Sir,

"I received your letter of 9th May. First of all, let me say that I am looking forward to my trip to the Burg. And then let me thank you for all the trouble you've had to give parents and boys this pleasure. The program has really been put up with so much care and consideration that it is likely to fulfill all wishes. Let us hope the weather will be good with plenty of sunshine and warmth, thus embellishing this meeting planned long ago. So, "Auf Wiedersehen," and let's hope that nothing will come in between.

"It has been my intention for some time to write to you but I did not want to do it before having your report on Horst in hand. I am so happy you are satisfied with the boy for I am convinced that he gives of his best and is fully conscious of duties and obligations. From one vacation to another I can notice the fitful development of the boy. Especially during the last vacation when I had more time to be together with the boy I could observe that his good characteristics became more prominent. You yourself acknowledge them. And that is what I wanted to write to you about: That here it is not a question of inheritance but that it shows the work of the teacher who knows his duty to make of these boys useful human beings for their people and country. For, after all, it is one of the most important tasks today to train human beings in whose hands one can lay the leadership of a nation. The National Socialistic conception of life is so logical that you cannot think of a world without it, but it has to be communicated in order to be solidly rooted within the German nation. How fortunate we must consider ourselves to have been born into this moment of eternal life and that we are part and parcel of the German people with the only Führer whom even other nations call a phenomenon, and that we may collaborate in his work. That's how I feel and you too, and that's why I am so thankful to you and your comrades that in your way of education you realize the idea (according to Rosenberg) taking shape. A splendid task to form these boys.

"Sometimes I, as a mother, am seized by an awful longing for the boy because you wish to implant into your child your way of feeling and thinking and to form and influence it according to your own perception. You will readily understand this. Then again, it is a great solace to know that our boy's in the best of hands when with you and that we serve in our place a purpose which may be more serious than we imagine, for the National Socialistic idea must never again be lost for us. Let us hope that when we parents meet you at the Burg, we shall have the occasion for a more serious exchange of thoughts.

"Till then, our kindest regards, also to Mr. ... Please give Horst my love.

"Heil Hitler! Yours ..."

"11th June 1939

My dear comrade,

"I wish to express to you again my heartiest thanks for the nice days which I was permitted to spend there.

"The Ordensburg, taking it as a whole, has made a great impression on me. How fortunate the boys may consider themselves to be permitted to live there and to be brought up—more than anything else—by such exemplary National Socialists. What a pity that I am not 15 years younger; I should love to go to an Ordensburg and start as a "Junker" (leader of youth). Pity, it can't be done now.

"I have had the experience of a nice patch of German soil and of "Sonthofen." My best thanks for it again, my dear comrade, to you, your wife, your comrades, who took troubles to make this visit by the parents a success.

"Kindest regards from my wife and myself. Heil Hitler! Yours ..."

CHAPTER FIVE

SONTHOFEN'S LAST DAYS

T he school functioned through the end of the war. But students and faculty fled with the approach of French forces in the spring of 1945.

On June 22, 1946, the deputy Burgermeister (Mayor) of Sonthofen gave the following chronological account of events that transpired from that time period up until the time American forces entered Sonthofen.

Deputy Burgermeister's Account[1]

"Almost up to the last phase of the war, the Upper Allgäu was a peaceful island amidst a devastating world conflagration, spared all warlike happenings save a few. Small wonder then when on April 27, 1945, toward 1:00 in the afternoon, the first enemy alarm was given. The population became restless and the direct realities of the war were brought home to the borough and its inhabitants.

"Human beings from far away, unfamiliar with our manners and ways, went plundering through our region, threatening the population, thus symbolizing the approaching collapse. Coolheaded men of our borough caused at the last minute that first of all no senseless resistance be offered and secondly, necessary foodstuffs and commodities for the coming anxious times be issued to the frightened population free of any ration cards.

"Life in the streets was motley and causing excitement and one could not free oneself of the feeling of emptiness when seeing parts of the once so popular "Wehrmacht" broken and split up during the flight on the highways. Deception and corruption were all around us.

"On Sunday, April 29th, 1945, the last attack of fighter planes swept over our borough. Our parish church, dwellings and business homes were laid waste in the last minutes of this senseless struggle.

Sonthofen church and retirement home bombed during 1945 air raid

"Finally the next day, April 30, 1945, at about 6:00 in the evening, the first French armored cars reached our borough. The Burgermeister at that time was Paul Herkommer, who handed over the town to the Second Morrocan Division of the French army in front of the old town hall. During an unusually heavy snow blizzard the French tricolor was hoisted on top of the old town hall—thus bringing to an end a full day of tension.

"During the night of April 30th, 1945, the building of the Landrat (hall of records), a former castle, was consumed by flames, burning down to the ground through a regrettable error on the part of the occupying troops who shot it on fire.

"A mob of robbers and plunderers marched through the streets of Sonthofen, causing great losses and damage until the French commander energetically put a stop to this evil and called these marauders to account. Placards by the French Occupation Force were stuck up in increasing numbers and ordinances told the population what was to be handed over to them—weapons, radios, and photo cameras were piling up in the council hall of the former town hall, when on May 3rd, 1945, at about 5:00 PM, a violent explosion caused by ammunition took place in the building, followed in the ensuing night by a conflagration completely destroying the former town hall. The two top officials of the former National Socialist Party of Sonthofen were arrested during the same night.

"The second Burgermeister since the end of the war was put into office by order of the occupational forces. At the same time a French civil commissioner was nominated, who was responsible for the orderly conduct of public life. A difficult time for making reparations followed.

"Valuable breeding cattle and many other goods went abroad; excesses of various kinds, by liberated foreign forced-labor hands, were of a daily order—the occupation troops and police forces found it difficult to cope with it all.

"On Sunday, May 20th, 1945, General Charles de Gaulle reviewed his troops in Obersdorf.

"Slowly but steadily time brought to the civilian population the peace that was so much longed for. Work was restarted everywhere and the stir and bustle everywhere indicated the coming of better times.

"Long before that the population talked about the imminent relief of French troops by American units. At the beginning of July, 1945, the first American troops reached Sonthofen and the last French troops left our borough. On Sunday, July 8th, 1945, the American military government took over.

"From July 8 1945 to June 1946:

"From that day onward life and the doings of our borough took a turn for the better. Trade and industry restarted their production as far as possible, with new hopes. The third Burgermeister took over the burdensome office in these days.

"Evacuated persons from all zones left the Allgaü which had offered them hospitality.

"The railroad and soon after the post office began to work again fully. The first transportation of essential commodities to cover the need of the local population were ordered. Notwithstanding crushing defeat and consequent dejection of the population, some silver lines became visible here and there. The first licensed newspaper informed the population of our borough of the happenings of the outer world.

"The first elections ordered by the military government cast the first highlights on the coming democratic renovation of the German provinces and boroughs. War crimes and misleading propaganda were demonstrated impartially to the population of the last 12 years. The political and public life is restarting everywhere in our borough.

"Now the fourth Burgermeister has taken over office as head of the community. The Localities (offices) of the market borough were taken together with the offices of the Landratsamt from the former occupants' 'Jager Kaserne' (Riflemen's Barracks), where they found simple but suitable accommodations. The larger part of the "Jager Kaserne" became a tuberculosis hospital for former soldiers of the German Wehrmacht. The former artillery barracks were taken over by UNRRA (United Nations Relief and Rehabilitation Administration) for DPs (Displaced Persons) and foreigners.

"Then the fifth Burgermeister took over his duties. The tuberculosis military hospital became a civilian hospital for tuberculosis patients and the artillery barracks was cleared out by UNRRA and the foreigners who left for MURNAU (a displaced persons camp mostly for Polish and Ukranian Displaced Persons.)

"January 1946:

"The former Ordensburg became a training school for American troops stationed in Germany. In the meantime fresh elections took place in Sonthofen which were actively attended and from which the Christian Social Union emerged as by far the strongest party with the largest concentration and a majority of the votes.

"Private dwelling houses were seized for purposes of the occupying forces. Fugitives (sic) from the east arrived and were expected, thus complicating the housing problem beyond measure. Notwithstanding, the good understanding between the population and the American troops was not spoiled.

"The sixth and so far the last Burgermeister was elected by the new town councilors on the basis of the preceding elections and is exercising his responsibility in office with much understanding for the citizens of Sonthofen.

"The arbitration courts (Spruchkammern) for de-Nazification will lead, it is expected, to a speedy pacification among all circles of the population; the seized houses were released (partly); a good crop is looked for, and the population hopes for a better future notwithstanding the present difficulties."

[End of Sonthofen's Deputy Burgermeister's account of the last days of the war, dated June 22, 1946]

CHAPTER SIX

PLANNING FOR THE OCCUPATION

In Early 1946, as the American press was questioning the wisdom of United States policy for the occupation of Germany, Gault MacGowan—a staff correspondent for the New York Sun—was granted a series of interviews with U.S. Army Maj. Gen. Ernest Harmon, who invited MacGowan to accompany him during his many inspection tours across the American occupation zone.

The interviews were conducted during the period of time when personnel shortages, caused by the rapid demobilization of American troops, were hindering the transition from war-footing to occupation. The brand-new U.S. Constabulary (responsible for administering the overall occupation of Germany, as well as physically patrolling the occupation zones and borders) had already begun training, and had graduated its first class from the new Constabulary School prior to the interviews.

Following are excerpts from articles based on those interviews, published in April of 1946 (obtained by this author through the generosity of the Norwich University Special Collections

Section of the Kreitzberg Library in Northfield, Vermont, where Gen. Harmon served as president from 1950-1965):

MacGowan, Gault, 'U.S. Constabulary in Reich Has First Asset of Glamour,' The New York Sun, Wednesday, April 24, 1946:
Bamberg,Germany, April 15th, 1946

"… 'The Constabulary is the pride of the Third Army,' Ritchie [Captain George Ritchie, public relations czar of the Third Army] told me before taking off—and after a few minutes with Harmon I found out why.

"The new task force has the glamour of the Texas Rangers for its recruits and the magnetism of a great experiment for the old campaigner, while for the top-ranking military mind it provides a tactical solution of the occupational problem that has possibilities of becoming strategical as well. But today, its problems are chiefly logistic and human.

"…No one who is not joining up with the Army on a permanent basis is being taken into the new force if he has a G.I. score of over forty points. This means that the general is working on a huge mass of raw material arrived in the past week or so as replacements from the United States—boys for the most part of the 18- to 20-year-old vintage just out of their first six weeks' military training.

"'I don't mind too much about that,' Harmon told me, 'We have an excellent training school for them, and they are all keen to serve in the new force and learn the inside dope on the new role in which they will function. Seventy percent of my organization will be new men from home. This represents terrific expansion, and we are very short of veterans and non-coms to train them. We have to train the men to train the newcomers. What training these young soldiers had at home was not in constabulary arms and equipment.'

"This new Constabulary demands the utmost versatility of its commander. It's to be a composite force of all arms from airplanes to tanks and riflemen, with some troopers— that's what they call the G.I.s now in the outfit—on horseback, some on motorcycles, some in automobiles of various types, including radio cars, and, eventually, some on skis. But, given the right commander, with the requisite understanding of all arms and their respective uses, the force promises to be the ideal instrument for occupational duties, and it is no secret that the French and British are watching its development closely.

"Harmon has no militant ambition for his force, but this burly, hearty, friendly ex-cavalryman and former chief of the hard-hitting Hell-on-Wheels Armored Division has a definite mission imposed on him by Gen. Joseph T. McNarney, theater commander, of preserving the security of the Constabulary empire they are carving out of Germany for him. Mainly, his mission will be to safeguard the regular garrison troops and see that McNarney's directives are carried out.

"This will be effected in a crosspatch of duties alternating between those of regular State police and the National Guard. They will serve sometimes as a National

Guard outfit in support of the German police which operate under the local military governments and burgermeisters. In times of emergency, they may be obliged to take over the German police duties altogether. But while things are normal they will run outpost duties and highway and border patrols much as the Texas Rangers or the Royal Canadian Mounties do.

"Up in the high mountains on the frontiers of the American Zone, mounted troopers will operate through the forest trails wherever jeeps cannot easily go. When the snows fall, ski troops may patrol the smugglers' paths, and if any Wehrwolf organization wants to start any mountain terrorism, Harmon will be ready for them with reinforcements of tanks and motorized troops moving out of central barracks in each of his Constabulary zones.

"'For this work,' Harmon told me, 'swift communications will be essential. Here again is a problem. How to get enough skilled radio operators in the short time left to train beginners? How do I get enough

Communications class at the Constabulary School

automotive mechanics to take care of my vehicles and airplanes?'"

"He needs 2,700 radio men and signalers and 1,700 mechanics. He outlined for me the intensive training scheme he has devised with special courses at Third Army schools or at the Constabulary 'West Point' he has created deep in the Bavarian Alps, in buildings that were a project of the late Robert Ley, the Nazi labor boss, and Baldur von Schirach, the Nazi youth leader. The Nazis planned to educate 'future leaders of the Third Reich.' Harmon chuckles when he thinks of the leaders that this school will produce now.

"There has been much talk of the way Germans are said to be losing respect for our occupation troops through the loose and unmilitary behaviour of some young soldiers and a few bored old ones in a country where military standards are closely watched and criticized by the most military-minded people in the world. Under a slogan of 'Mobility! Vigilance! Justice!' Harmon plans to correct this impression, and naughty G.I.s of the future who do things they shouldn't oughta will have to watch their step when Harmon's Hardboots are on patrol.

"Trouble between the G.I. and the German is of constant occurrence. I had scarcely left the General when I heard of a German car, halted with a 'flat' on a lonely country road, having all its windows smashed by a Joe with an itchy rifle butt. Apparently the job was done on the general principle of antipathy for Nazis; the unfortunate thing was that, as too frequently happens, the Joe was not selective in his measures. For the car drivers concerned, with official permission to use an automobile, were high-ranking members of the Christian Democratic Party.

"All is not fraternization in Germany, though judging by the headline high spots, the average citizen at home might justifiably think so sometimes. Harmon cannot keep his own eye on every such incident, but by dispersal of a part of his force to be his ears and eyes throughout the American Zone of occupation, he hopes to keep in close contact with everything that is going on aboveground and underground.

"He will police an area roughly 300 by 250 miles in extent, or more than one-and-a-half times the size of the entire State of New York. He will have 38,000 men to do the job with, somewhere about the strength of three divisions. To visit and inspect all his outfits scattered all over Robin Hood's barn, takes him days of travel weekly.

"'I am running myself to death even now,' he told me, 'and we are not yet operative. I have thirty-nine tactical units to inspect at present. On my last trip, I saw twenty and I traveled 5,400 miles. When I go on my next trip, come with me and I will show you what I mean.'"

MacGowan, Gault, 'Goering's Special Train Is Now Gen. Harmon's Lightning Bolt,' The New York Sun, Thursday, April 25, 1946:
Speeding Through Germany, April 16th, 1946

"I am writing this dispatch aboard Goering's special

train, sitting in the Diesel locomotive cab beside the German driver, and this is one German train I won't jump out from—just now she's moving at 100 miles an hour. We slow down now and then to cross over some temporary span that German railroaders have put in to repair bridges blown up by the Wehrmacht (German Armed Forces) when fighting was on. It's awe-inspiring sometimes to look out and see through gaps in the timber bridging a silver stream tumbling over a rocky riverbed far below. But—so far—we have negotiated all these hazards.

"Every now and then the driver looks at his watch and checks his position against a schedule laid out before him as we flash by a wayside station. A minute too soon or a minute too late and he adjusts speed so as to be dead on time at his next check point.

"It's midnight. The track ahead is lit up by our headlights—and a full moon silhouettes the tall trees and forests along the track. Sitting the other side of the engineman—a stranger in these parts—is a pilot engineman who knows every inch of the track we are going over and warns the driver when to take it easy and when he can safely put on speed. We change the pilot at every divisional point to make sure we have always a man who really knows the track.

"Behind us, keeping an earnest eye on the twelve-cylinder Diesels, is Karl Wick, a veteran who has been on this flyer ever since it got its picture in the German illustrated weeklies as a Nazi ground effort to compete with air travel organizations between South Germany and

Berlin. He had run this train for Goering and his high-ranking Luftwaffe friends for about four years before the United States Army co-opted it into our scheme of High Command communications.

"We are on our way to pick up Major Gen. Ernest N. Harmon, chief of the new United States Army Constabulary, who will use it for a staff headquarters while inspecting a succession of scattered outfits. He will sleep in Goering's outsize suite, lined in satinwood, and will cool off in his marble shower. The general, however, does not expect the versatility of this 240-foot speed job that Goering demanded. Goering had it fixed so that the train would run forward or backward, which must have been disconcerting to any of our American flyers who tried to shoot it up. It's another twelve-cylinder Diesel at the back of the train that makes this trick possible.

"All it does for Gen. Harmon and his staff is to speed up their inspection tours. They don't have to bother shunting around or switching engines when they want to return to their headquarters. The crew just drives the train home backwards. On board are sleeping accommodations for eighteen of us, and there's a dining car and a lounge.

"A German chef does wonders with United States Army rations. All in all, we have the ideal mobile headquarters for a general commanding one of the most dispersed and scattered forces the United States has owned for many generations. The general can eat and sleep while traveling and save hours of daylight for inspecting purposes.

"The railroads in the American zone were turned back

to the Germans last January with orders to get them going for military traffic and with permission to use them again for authorized civilian transportation. Farsightedly, some one reserved this flyer for military purposes and named it officially U.S. 4. It is generally referred to now as Harmon's Lightning Bolt. And a lightning bolt, bye the bye, is on the new Constabulary shoulder patch.

"Capt. Arthur E. Wright of the Army Transportation Corps is the train chief and resident manager aboard. A former Ohio schoolteacher, he has been railroading now for about two years and claims he has had about $1,000,000 worth of travel at Uncle Sam's expense.

"He explained to me how our present journey was scheduled: 'Gen. Harmon just said where and when he wanted to go. His staff worked out the arrival sequences and the German railroaders set the schedule to have us every place the general wanted to go on time. With usual German efficiency, they seem to get us to every location on the minute!'"

MacGowan, Gault, 'Harmon and Staff Keep Touch With new Reich Unit by Train,' The New York Sun, Wednesday, April 24, 1946:
Aboard the Lightning Bolt, Germany, April 17th, 1946

"Major Gen. Ernest N. Harmon's flier travels through the American Occupation Zone like a presidential train. All the key members of his staff—or their deputies—are with him writing up their reports for his study and review after each wayside halt.

"I am the first correspondent to accompany the general on one of these trips which he has been making regularly since late in February.

"...You might think there was all the equipment in the world over here to outfit the new force effectively. But that was before we turned over huge dumps and barns full of brand new equipment to the British, the French, the Belgians and the Czechs on one political agreement or another. As it is, the new force is dependent on what has been turned in by home-bound divisions or deactivated armies.

"Much of this is war-worn and war-torn and badly in need of overhauling, but as most of the expert war technical

General Harmon inspecting 6th Constabulary Squadron vehicles

corpsmen have gone home with high pointage, there has just not been the staff here to do such work. Lots of equipment, tanks, trucks, armored cars, jeeps, have been left for weeks only roughly protected against the elements in open fields and parking lots in the absence of any undercover barns to keep them in this devastated Germany.

"A brand new force like the Constabulary—which aims to be a corps d'elite—deserves brand new weapons, but there is little prospect now of their getting them. I have seen tanks and armored cars turned over to them that will require weeks of work to make road-worthy. And before they can begin the work, mechanics have to be trained by the Constabulary or the Army to do the job. The shortage of specialists over here is crucial.

"Redeployment on the point system has taken no account of a man's individual value to the Army. The theory that no man is indispensable and that the draft can always effect a replacement, has been carried to a perplexing extreme for those responsible for the swift efficiency of the new force.

"This staff train tour of the scattered Constabulary force brings the personal contact of its master minds with the executive officers responsible for carrying out the volumes of directives from the Army chiefs. As we stopped today at wayside stations I sat in with the chiefs of each section in succession and heard them listen to the troubles of the local executive officers and help them with advice and sympathy. We average about an hour at each halt. As the train drew into the station the general and his staff stepped smartly out and into waiting motorcars.

"Within a few minutes each staff chief was consulting with his opposite number in the outfit concerned while the general toured around talking with and encouraging the men and watching them at work.

"In one hour stop at one station I watched a horsed

General Harmon inspecting Headquarters Troop and Medical Detachment 6th Squadron

cavalry drill, recruit riflemen learn to shoot and dismantle weapons, men working on tanks, armored cars, trucks and motorcycles and 18-year-old boys who had never seen a radio transmitter a few weeks ago learning to send the Morse code. In a twelve-weeks' course they will be expected to send and receive radio messages at twelve words a minute. This is a very slow rate compared with commercial transmissions, but the Constabulary thinks they will be able to get by with it until these new troopers have gained more experience. Anyhow, there is nothing they can do about it, as all the real experts in radio have long since gone home.

"The general told me tonight that he was very pleased with what he had seen and that despite all the difficulties in building a new and experimental force good progress is being made. He is confident that when D-day dawns for the Constabulary to take over they will be ready to do so with efficiency, dignity and credit to itself and the Army."

MacGowan, Gault, 'U.S. Constabulary Hunting For Nazi Secrets in the Alps,' the New York Sun: Lenggries, Austrian Border, April 18th

"As Major Gen. Harmon's special train pulls into this frontier station cradled in spurs of the Alps, a smart honor guard springs to attention. A brief ceremony, an eagle-eyed inspection of men and equipment and the guard falls out at the double to tumble into armored cars to escort the Constabulary chief and his staff officers into town.

"I ride in the second automobile behind the general and his aide. Major John Millikin, twenty-seven year-old son of Maj. Gen. Millikin and grandson of Gen. Peyton C. March, the Gen. Marshall of World War I, command this outfit… formed out of the Second United States Cavalry. He has it set up in white barracks formerly a training school for SS non-coms. On the big parade ground, his men are drawn up to show the general what a crack Constabulary outfit can look like on parade. With Lieut. Warren F. Bradeen from Missoula, Mont., I go to inspect the Intelligence Division—G-2—and to learn the secrets of what goes on behind these mysterious Alps.

"I learn that we haven't had time yet to tooth-comb these mountains. But the Constabulary is beginning to do it. At daybreak they drive high into an Alpine valley; then they break up into small parties, and each taking a mountain slope march on an azimuth, where they will rendezvous for supper. Usually, it's a fifteen- to twenty-mile hike for the mountain patrols, stimulated by the champagne-like air and the thrill of meeting strange people and unexpected situations. For this is hillbilly country, where people scarcely know there has been a war on, have missed the full impact of Allied control and have never been to town to read the proclamations of military government.

"Alpine chalets are being thoroughly searched now, on mountain after mountain; identity papers are being carefully checked and suspects rounded up. Though at the end of the war hunts for wanted Nazis were pursued through the Alps, I have not heard of anything quite so intensive as this before. Constabulary troopers plan to know every cave and every possible cache in their area.

"If the order ever comes to close the Austro-Bavarian frontier they will be able to do it, fortified with the knowledge of every smuggler's path and every chamois hunter's nest."

CHAPTER SEVEN

PREPARING THE CONSTABULARY SCHOOL

During the period that Gen. Harmon and his staff were conducting occupation-zone inspections, select military personnel in the European theater (whose skills and specialties were needed for the opening of the school at Sonthofen) were reassigned to assist in preparing for the arrival of the first class.

One of the first to arrive in Sonthofen in January, 1946, was U.S. Army Sgt. Charles Hughes and his group of specialists from C Battery, 630th Field Artillery Battalion. Hughes was responsible for training aids and the new film library, among other duties. In a personal letter to the author, Hughes writes:

"When we arrived at the building that was assigned to us, our sleeping quarters were on the second floor. We had quite a bit of cleaning to do before we could get our equipment installed. The rooms were large and contained a lot of furniture and many drafting tables. We found discarded plans and blueprints with drawings of rocket parts."

It was discovered that a secret facility in Sonthofen produced parts that were installed in German rockets. Many of the Hitler Youth at the School volunteered their time and assistance at this facility.

Hughes continues:

"When I received my assignment, I also learned that some of the talented people I was working with would accompany me to Sonthofen. They included three young soldiers, a Hungarian Displaced Person, and a Russian girl named Olgar, who were all outstanding artists.

"Our first major assignment was to paint the Constabulary emblem on all the helmet liners for the school staff and permanent personnel. We worked many hours and were happy that we were able to complete the task in time for the first incoming class of students. Our next assignment was to undertake the drawing, painting and production of training charts and visual aid posters for the various departments at the school. One school department had us make charts and posters of the Nuremburg war crime trials that were in progress at the time."

An elaborate and extensive Professional Training Aids Dept. was eventually developed at the school. Thousands of charts became available to the academic departments in addition to many forms of training aids, resulting in more impressive and meaningful instruction for the students.

Hughes continues:

"A month after arriving, I had one of my most interesting experiences that took place one evening while I was in charge of quarters. General Harmon arrived in his chauffeured sedan. After asking me if everything was going well, we began to chat and he told me he had been on an inspection tour on the eastern border of the occupation zone. I offered him a cup of coffee, and he began talking about the school and how pleased he was that the training and educational programs were progressing. I only learned much later that he was one of the most decorated generals in the U.S. Army."

On Jan. 15, 1946, the Second Cavalry Squadron arrived in Sonthofen to take command of the former Hitler Youth School complex. The squadron's mission was to relieve the 14th Infantry and organize the facility for classes. The troopers began by securing items that had not yet arrived for the permanent school staff: billets, furniture and equipment.

Private Ray Rempe of A Company, 2nd Cavalry Reconnaissance Squadron, was a member of the contingent, which in early January 1946, made the trip to Sonthofen from the town of Schwabach located south of Nuremberg.

In a letter, Rempe writes:

"We were told that we would have to get the school cleaned and operational for the first class of students arriving in early March, as the facility had become the new Training and Educational Center for the United States Constabulary. At the end of the day, in our spare time, some of my buddies and I would explore the huge facility and on one trip discovered tunnels under some buildings. We learned that during the construction of the Hitler Youth School, underground tunnels were built that connected all of the buildings.

"One day a few of us decided to explore those underground tunnels. We found storage areas with old discarded Hitler Youth uniforms scattered around. In another section of the tunnel we found what appeared to be a medical laboratory where we found several large glass containers with human baby fetuses in formaldehyde. It appeared that research of some type had been carried on but I could never find out anything more about it. We came out of the tunnel at the far end of a quadrangle, and on the east side of the buildings was a children's nursery. There were children ranging from one year to about five years old being cared for by German nurses. We questioned the nurses about the children and were informed they were the offspring of the female employees (mostly the waitresses) that worked in the dining facility.

"The next time I went to the dining hall I talked to one of the waitresses about what I had seen. She informed me that many of the children's fathers were members of the Nazi teaching staff, SS officers who had since fled. She also told me that during their pregnancies they were encouraged and paid to continue working at the Hitler Youth School.

There are many stories about activities that went on during the height of Nazi power at the Hitler Youth School. Sonthofen was the site of many high-level Nazi Party Conferences, as well as social events that would bring together staff personnel with young women from other party organizations. It's not too difficult to understand the nationalistic pride that prevailed in Germany at that time. We will never know the full extent of events that took place or programs implemented at the site of the school in Sonthofen. The destruction and burning of files by SS troops during the last days of the war has only deepened the mystery. Most people were reluctant to even talk about it.

CHAPTER EIGHT

THE NEWTON TOUCH

In late January 1946, the 465th Anti-Aircraft Automatic
Weapons Battalion was notified that it was to relieve the 2nd
Cavalry group in Sonthofen. The battalion was to become the
"designated" unit to operate the new Constabulary School. Under
the command of Lt. Col. Fredrick W. Ledeboer, the battalion left
Heilbron (near Heidelberg) and arrived at the school on February
12, 1946.

Col. Harold G. Holt, the newly named "commandant" of the
school, and his staff immediately reorganized the battalion into a
unit that would meet the necessary requirements for the operation
and administration of the school. (On May 1, the battalion would
be re-designated the Constabulary School Squadron.)

On Feb. 18, Col. Henry C. Newton arrived at the new
U.S. Constabulary School to assume his duties as assistant
commandant and director of training. Newton had served at the
Armored Force Training Center, Fort Knox, Kentucky in early
1940, conducting considerable research in armored infantry

Colonel Henry C. Newton, Assistant Commandant, U.S. Constabulary School

tactics. He was also founder and director of the Armored Forces Officers School Training Center at Fort Knox. The Center—well-known in the armored forces as the school for officers of all grades learning the finer points of armored warfare—was affectionately referred to as "Newton's College." And by war's end, more than 3,000 officers had become Newton graduates.

Newton, however, was eager for and requested overseas service, accepting a special assignment in the European theater, where he served on the general staff of Supreme Headquarters Allied Expeditionary Forces. In 1945, he was temporarily detached to Allied Forces Headquarters Mediterranean Theater of Operations, where he was tasked with coordinating a special operation.

On June 10, Newton became director and commandant of the Ministerial Collection Center near Kassel, Germany, an intelligence operation involving the collection and evaluation of intelligence documents, manuscripts and the like that had been seized by U.S. forces. Newton served in this capacity until Feb 12, 1946, at which time he was reassigned to the Constabulary School in Sonthofen.

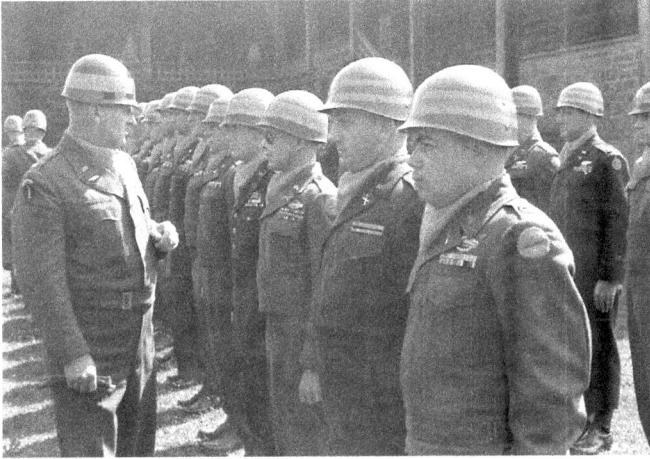

Colonel Newton conducts inspection of Constabulary School department heads

Days after Newton's Feb. 18 arrival at the Constabulary School, the old Newton College touch began to be felt throughout all departments and sections of the school. With only two weeks until the arrival of the first class, proposed lesson plans were under constant review and revision; rewrites were frequent.

All departments in the Academic Division that were to be directly involved in the day-to-day teaching were required to participate in a series of instructors' courses to improve presentation skills and teaching techniques, under Newton's direct supervision. He was especially concerned that after four weeks of intensive study and training the graduates would be able to return to their units as fully capable instructors.

FIRST CLASS BEGINS

On March 4, the first class of selected officers and enlisted men to attend the U.S. Constabulary School arrived to begin their four weeks of intensive study and training.

Throngs of field grade officers, enrolled in the school's special

*Special 3-day
orientation
course
briefing for
Field Grade
Officers*

three-day orientation courses, began flying into the school's airfield. Once on the ground, those officers barely had time to leave their bags in their quarters before the program began, which would crash-familiarize them with the overall curriculum and training activities slated to be taught to the Constabulary students.

The first class, composed of 532 students, was welcomed by the new school commandant Col. Holt, who introduced the new commanding general, Maj. Gen. Harmon. In his welcoming remarks, Harmon reminded students of why they were there,

*Orientation
for new
student
body*

and the fact that each man had been selected by virtue of his ability to learn quickly and to be able to transfer their newly acquired knowledge to others. High standards of personal appearance, military courtesy, and discipline were also expected and demanded.

During that first week it was not unusual to find Newton visiting classrooms and training grounds: observing teaching methods, student formations, and riot-control demonstrations. In one instance shortly after the arrival of the second class—

Students listen to welcoming address by School Commandant

during an unannounced visit to the gym where students were learning search procedures, as well as judo and unarmed defense techniques—Newton interrupted the class to praise the officers and tell them how impressed he was with both the instructors and the students. (The author, who was present at the time, recalls how high morale was following the visit.)

In June of 1948, Newton was named commandant of the Constabulary School, succeeding Colonel Theodore E. Buechler.

CHAPTER NINE

BASIC TRAINING TO SONTHOFEN
THE AUTHOR'S STORY

On November 3, 1945, six months after graduation, 17-year-old John Capone walked into the U.S. Army recruiting office in New Haven, Conn., and announced to the recruiting officer that he wanted to join the Army. Ever since that war started, Capone says, "I felt a patriotic duty to serve my country."

Since I was only 17, my mother had to sign the enlistment papers, which she did while crying. The recruiter informed me that I could choose any branch of service and any theater of operations I wanted. I decided to join the infantry and selected the European Theater of Operations. After a physical, some processing, swearing-in, and receipt of a seven-day pass, I boarded a train bound for Fort McClellan, Alabama and 90 days of basic training.

Army training in 1945 was tough: hours of daily close order drill, obstacle courses, calisthenics, rifle cleaning, marksmanship and bayonet training, 10-mile marches, gas mask training, throwing hand grenades, firing bazookas at tanks, and constant classroom instruction.

Near the end of training, we were told that replacements were urgently needed overseas to replace war-weary veterans who were on the verge of rioting. Training was cut short, and after a brief trip home to say "goodbyes," I was ordered to Fort Dix, New Jersey, and from there to Germany.

SONTHOFEN

It was March 14, 1946 when I finally arrived in Sonthofen from the Marburg (Germany) processing center. I was told that I was being assigned to a new "peacekeeping force" being organized that would be called the United States Constabulary. Eight other recruits made the trip with me.

En route to Sonthofen—riding in the back of a two-and-a-half ton truck—I remember passing through city after city of utter devastation and destruction; there were miles of rubble as far as the eye could see, with only the occasional church steeple piercing the sky above the ruins.

As we approached Munich, we saw women standing in the middle of the ruins surrounded by bombed-out shells of buildings. The women were cleaning and chipping away at huge piles of brick salvaged from those buildings as well as structures that had been completely flattened.

Around noon we stopped in Munich at one of the Army mess kitchens, where we ate heartily and took a great deal of ribbing from the combat soldiers who were waiting to go home. I was happy to get back on the truck and on our way. An hour or so beyond Munich we were in the heart of Lower Bavaria with its beautiful vistas and few if any signs of the war that had destroyed so much of the rest of the country.

It was late afternoon when we arrived in Sonthofen. We were driven to the former German Jager Kaserne—artillery barracks (located on the outskirts of town near the Iller River) that were being used as a motor pool and provost marshal's headquarters. There we were assigned to temporary barracks, stowed our gear, and began in-processing.

Two days later, processing completed, I received orders to Academic Troop, Constabulary School Squadron Special Troops. And so—along with two other soldiers—I was transported up a long winding road to the school.

At the Constabulary School, I was surprised to find our quarters better than most college dorms I had seen at Yale University. We received an orientation by First Sgt. Elmer H. Hector, and were welcomed by our company commander, Capt. James W. Speers, who reminded us that the success of the occupation depended on each of us doing our jobs in a professional manner.

The following morning, my long-awaited assignment was posted on the company bulletin board. I was ordered to report to the Department of General Subjects, which taught search procedures, unarmed defense, judo, and physical training. I reported to the gym to begin training.

Classes had been underway for 10 days, and because I lacked any formal training, I was not permitted to teach right away. I was assigned to another instructor, Staff Sgt. Frank Broce. The following two weeks were spent in an intensive training program under the direction of Lt. Daniel Herman, provost marshal.

Unarmed defense class

We took advantage of whatever free time we had between classes to practice, and on many evenings a few of us would go to the gym to work on what we had learned that day. By the end of the second week we began to develop our skills on disarming a potential enemy, search procedures, judo flips, and various other close combat techniques. We often held competitions among ourselves.

CHAPTER TEN

"A SOLDIER IS A TEACHER"
Sonthofen Graduates its First Class

On March 28, 1946, the first class of officers and enlisted men was graduated from the "Constabulary West Point." One hundred twenty-two officers and 364 enlisted men, all hand-

Constabulary School Graduation

picked, completed instructor courses ranging from geopolitics and elements of crime and border control to communications.

With the snow-capped peaks of the Bavarian Alps as a backdrop, Maj. Gen. Harmon addressed the graduating class, which was assembled in Stotsenburg Quadrangle. A transcript of Harmon's speech follows:

"The graduation today of the first class to attend the Constabulary School is a definite landmark in the progress of the development of the United States Constabulary. The organization of the school, the development of the courses of instruction, the assembly of the instructors and students, were all accomplished under the most difficult situation and in a very short period of time. It is an outstanding achievement and one of which I am very proud and in which all of you people who took part and worked so hard can have great satisfaction.

"The Constabulary School is more than a place of instruction. It is the cradle, so to speak, in which we hope to establish the character, the esprit de corps, and high standards of personal conduct and appearance of the Constabulary.

"While you have been here you have been required to give your most earnest and intensive effort. The course has been short in duration. We fully realize that the time has not been sufficient to thoroughly master all the subjects. A choice had to be made between quality and quantity at this stage of the development of the Constabulary.

"As most of the subjects taught here are entirely new

Classroom
Instructions

to the soldier and the normal training given to the soldier, it was felt necessary to obtain as quickly as possible the maximum number of graduates to act as instructors to their units and to spread the Constabulary standards and principles among their comrades. As time goes on we expect to strive for more quality in the results of instruction by lengthening the courses and also to provide new subjects of instruction.

"The Constabulary School serves as a library and a source of material for the training of all units. As time goes on we expect the School to be a laboratory, so to speak, for the development of the Constabulary technique and the means by which and through which the approved Constabulary doctrines and methods of employment will be disseminated throughout the command as a whole. A soldier is forever a teacher. 'When the teacher has taught well, the learner can perform.' The graduates of the school should remember the technique of teaching as taught here and should try to apply it when teaching their own schools or instructing the men in their units.

"These are difficult days for the soldier, particularly the professional soldier. During the war, there was nothing too good for the soldier, but as soon as the war ended, it always seems to be followed by a wave of criticism and lack of appreciation of the soldier. All of the petty little gripes are brought to the surface, and in the minds of many people, the great sacrifices and devotion to duty, particularly of the officers and those who held positions of great responsibility, are lost sight of. We hear much of the "caste system," of the belittling of officers. We hear charges that our army is undemocratic and the army has suffered by the thoughtless and disparaging statements of many of our soldiers toward their officers. During this war we developed a fine fighting army, and in my opinion, the most democratic army of the world. Over 800,000 officers were responsible for this army and operated it. Of this number over 500,000 rose to the grade of officer from the enlisted ranks. Certainly an army which offers such opportunity as this to its soldiers

Student Officer Corps

must be a democratic army.

"It takes time to develop an officer. There is much an officer should learn. Of so many thousands of new officers, there were many who made mistakes and who had not learned the art, and it is an art, of handling their men properly. There were many officers who made the mistake of thinking only of RHIP, or 'rank has its privileges.' It takes time for an officer to realize that RHIP must take second place in importance to RHIR, or 'rank has its responsibilities.' When the responsibility part is well carried out and practiced, when the officer develops the ability to take care of his men properly and has always on his mind and in his heart their best welfare, he really becomes an officer in fact as well as in name. No thinking soldier ever begrudges him what little privileges he may have. In fact, some of the greatest comforts and privileges that I have ever had as an officer throughout my career have been voluntarily given, though that they should do something to me by the men themselves who for me in return for what I have done for them. Let us not forget our duties as officers and non-commissioned officers.

"For more than a year before the end of the war there arose a great question in the minds of our countrymen concerning our ability to win what people came to call the 'Peace.' Now almost a year after the war has ended, that question is still unanswered. In many parts of Europe and Asia, and even in our own western hemisphere, there prevails enough unrest to leave most of us in doubt as to exactly what is in store for the world in the near future. In addition to the serious international problems, we here in Germany are faced with the problem of seeing that for once and for all time the hatred and tyranny of Nazism does not rise again. On us will rest a large share of the responsibility of assuring the security of the American occupational forces and that the policies of our government relative to the control and government of Germany in the American Zone are carried out. That is not going to be an easy task. The Constabulary will be a force of only about 38,000 men. We must see that the dignity of the United States of America is upheld in meeting our occupational duties. We must do this job and do it well in order that we will be regarded in the light of public opinion the same as that of another small group of men of whom the great British statesman, Winston Churchill, once said, 'Never did so many owe so much to so few.'

"We must not forget that we will be part of the answer to the question of winning the peace. We must see to it that this answer never remains in doubt through any failure on our part to meet the daily tasks that confront us here in Germany. Today you are the closest approach to what we hope the Constabulary trooper and officer will be. You know more about what your job is to be than any other class of personnel now in the Constabulary, and while here at school, you have lived and carried yourselves closest to the standards desired in the Constabulary than any other people we now have.

"Hold on to what you have acquired here, and when you go out to your units and meet the reinforcements who are now pouring in, carry on the instructions and standards you have acquired.

"Eventually you will be equipped with the best and in the most modern manner for the performance of your task, but in the final analysis it is the men who use the equipment that counts the most. Remember the motto of the Constabulary, 'Mobility, Vigilance and Justice.' We will be mobile by virtue of our vehicles; we must be vigilant by virtue of our minds and hearts. The character of our country and our training in its principles will insure that justice will be done in the performance of our duties. On the first of July the responsibility for the police and security of the American Zone rests squarely on us: The American Army, yes, the entire world, is waiting to see how we will perform.

"When I was a football player at the military academy, we used to have certain selected officers give us a pep talk before we left the dressing room to go out on the field to play the Navy, and I always remember and still get a thrill with the words that one of them said: 'From the rockbound coast of Maine, from the steaming jungles of Panama, from the sandy wastes of the Rio Grande, from the coral shores of Hawaii, the eyes of the Army are on you today.' We will have a greater audience.

"Our Constabulary is in much the same position as the troops of Napoleon when the whole world was watching as they started their march through the difficult passes of the Alps on to the plains of Italy. At that time Napoleon said, 'The snows of one hundred centuries are looking down on you.' I know you will perform well. I wish you Godspeed, and the best of luck."

Immediately upon the conclusion of the graduation ceremony, the graduates boarded vehicles to return to their units, and new students began to arrive. This process continued every four weeks.

Course material was updated constantly to keep pace with new experiences gained in the field, and changes took place daily. The school dropped certain courses and added others. The most significant changes occurred in police subjects, which became

European Armed Forces staff officers participating in School Graduation

the most important element of Constabulary operations.

Throughout 1946 and early 1947, when Constabulary student classes were at their peak, school personnel experienced many of the ceremonial functions that took place from month to month. Staff officers from the European Armed Forces Command usually delivered speeches to the student officers and enlisted men on graduation day, often paying tribute to the students and men of the United States Constabulary forces for achieving high standards in subject matter, personal appearance and discipline.

On graduation days—as new graduates returned to their units—the faculty almost always received a three-day pass. The most popular pass destination was Garmisch-PartenKirchen, the site of the 1933 Winter Olympics, where the Army in 1946-47 maintained the largest recreational facilities in Europe. The town, situated at the foot of the Zugspitze—the highest peak in Germany—was the site of the Army's recreational ski school (for members of the armed forces and their families).

On my very first visit, I decided I was going to learn to ski, so I enrolled in a beginner course. After a long day or two on the slopes, I met another soldier, Steve Papalos, who was stationed at the Supreme Headquarters Allied Powers Europe (SHAPE) in Frankfurt, where Gen. Dwight Eisenhower's headquarters were located. The buildings—former headquarters of I.G. Farben, the world's largest chemical conglomerate—were not bombed during the war. Rumor was, the buildings were spared on Ike's orders, because the general planned to locate Allied headquarters in the facilities.

When our skiing weekend was over, before I returned to the school, Papalos invited me to Frankfurt to visit SHAPE headquarters. Four weeks later, after the next series of student courses had ended, I made arrangements to visit Frankfurt.

Most of the city had been completely destroyed, but the heavily guarded SHAPE HQ was untouched. After a brief tour of SHAPE, Papalos and I spent the rest of the day driving around the city. Following dinner that evening at the SHAPE dining hall, we went to the Enlisted Men's Club.

The next morning, Papalos drove me to the train station at Frankfurt Au Main. As I entered the station to wait for my train to Sonthofen, I witnessed hundreds of Germans gathered at the far end of the terminal. When I inquired as to what was going on, I was told that the people were awaiting the arrival of the first German prisoners of war released by the Russians. The prisoners were part of the German Sixth Army that had fought in the disastrous (for the Germans) battle of Stalingrad during that terrible winter of 1942-43.

The train arrived with several hundred of the released prisoners: Men hobbled from the cars, dressed in ragged remnants of clothing, missing arms, missing legs, most on crutches with sack cloth covering their feet, bandages covering wounded heads and bodies. There was not a healthy-looking one in the bunch, and there were hundreds of them. The anguished women were screaming and crying as they searched the faces of the men to see if any were their loved ones.

Words cannot adequately describe the shock I felt witnessing this event. The pain and suffering all around me was indescribable.

I learned years later that of the 100,000 prisoners the Soviet Army had taken at Stalingrad, only 10,000 were released, most of them with crippling injuries. The Russians released the last group of German prisoners in 1955. When the German government questioned the Soviets as to the whereabouts of the remaining prisoners, the Soviets replied, "That's all we had."[1]

On April 29, 1946—almost one year to the day (April 30, 1945) after Hitler committed suicide—Col. John J. Binns was named Commandant of the Constabulary School. He replaced

Col. Holt, who was leaving the school to assume command of the 15th Constabulary Regiment. A graduate of West Point, Binns had deployed to Europe during the war with the VII Corps and commanded the 188th Field Artillery Group. Binns would now guide the school through its most intensive period of growth.

U.S. Constabulary School Commandant, Colonel John J. Binns

CHAPTER ELEVEN
THE MAKING OF A TROOPER

On any "Day One" for a new student at the Constabulary School, he was reminded of Gen. Harmon's words in his message to the Constabulary Forces on March 11, 1946, in which he stated:

"A high standard of discipline and achievement will be demanded; however, the work will be varied and interesting. Members of the Constabulary will feel great satisfaction in knowing that they are to take an important place in the organization that is to maintain the peace, the results won in war."

Upon completion of in-processing, the student was assigned to a student squadron, his primary unit. Each student squadron was organized into troops and platoons, with student officers in command of each troop and a non-commissioned officer leading each platoon.

Students were inspected in ranks twice daily to assure that standards of neatness and personal appearance were maintained. Faculty advisors were assigned to each troop and assisted the squadron commander with inspections. Breaches of discipline or failure to respond to corrections were reported to the student squadron commander for disciplinary action. Each night an officer from the faculty would make the necessary bed checks

Student
Formation

and other inspections. Emphasis was on personal appearance, courtesy, cleanliness of each trooper, care of equipment and attention to detail. Haircuts were required once a week.

While in the dining hall the senior non-commissioned officer at each table—the "table commandant"—was responsible for table manners, conservation of food, and general conduct of students at his table. Food was served by a staff of professional waitresses on the same porcelain plates, bowls, and silverware used to feed the previous occupants (Hitler Youth students and SS staff) while German musicians played classical music for the U.S. Army students. At the conclusion of the meal, the table commandant remained seated until his table was inspected by assigned mess personnel.

The topic of conversation was almost always the spectacular dining hall with its dramatically high ceilings featuring hand-carved wood panels (carved by local craftsmen in 1937). One of the largest such facilities in Europe, the dining hall could

Dining Hall

accommodate up to 1,500 students at one sitting. The vista looking out from the enormous floor-to-ceiling windows was absolutely breathtaking, with the snow-covered Allgaü mountain range in the background. It was not unusual to see deer grazing on the nearby hills and ridges.

Proper uniforms were required in all service clubs, post clubs, the library and other locations. All caps were removed and uniforms buttoned up upon entering. All brass, belt buckles, and insignias were highly polished, daily. Fatigues were not authorized in these locations, and the requirements were strictly enforced as part of the training and education of each student.

At 6:15 a.m. first call was sounded over the public address system to begin the student day. At 6:30 a.m. a 105 mm "salute" gun was fired and was followed by the sound of reveille. The

Marching to classrooms

school had numerous washrooms on each floor immediately adjacent to all living quarters so that shaving and showering before breakfast could be completed in a short time.

Mess was at 6:45 a.m. in a 1,500-man dining hall. After breakfast, students returned to and cleaned up their quarters, grabbed their field manuals and notebooks, and hurried to the first squadron formation of the day (7:48 am). Following inspection, the platoon marched off to its first class, arriving just before school call was sounded (8:00 am).

The majority of the troopers attended the enlisted men's basic course. A typical school day for an enlistee had him

Classroom instruction

participating in a Geopolitics Department lecture at 8:00 a.m., learning German history and how the Nazis came to power. At 8:50 a.m., troopers moved out with their platoon, assembling just outside the classroom building. Roll was called again and the platoon marched at attention to the next classroom. If time allowed, there was a "smoke break."

By 9:00 a.m. the platoon was again seated, and an officer from the Department of Public Safety might be discussing the

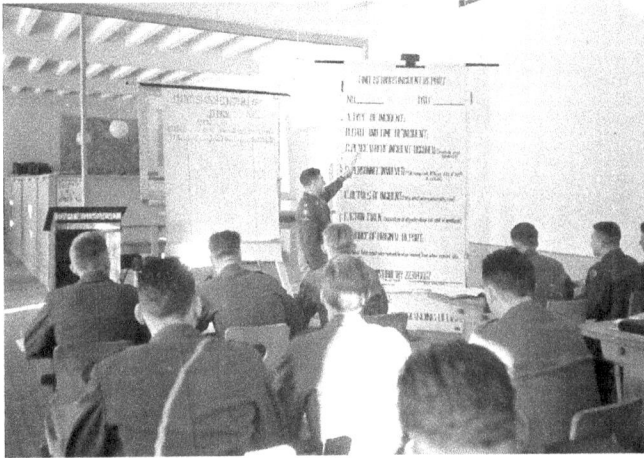

Classroom instruction

elements of crime or criminal investigations. The platoon then moved on to the Department of Tactics where two hours were devoted to border control methods and procedures, tactics of raids, search methods, and patrolling.

All platoons had "home rooms" where instruction was given for more than one period. Platoons moved out to the walk or porches for a 10-minute break at the end of each hour. At 11:50 a.m. the platoon was marched to barracks and dismissed for lunch.

Student troopers heard first call again at 12:45 and hurried to fall in before assembly sounded at 12:48. They were inspected by a faculty officer and then marched to their first afternoon class.

The scheduled class at 1:00 p.m. was Unarmed Defense, which was always a welcome break from the mental exercises of the classroom. The trooper now dressed in coveralls and gym shoes and learned the fundamentals of defending himself

Student Judo Demonstration by S/Sgt John Capone and S/Sgt Frank Broce

in a close-quarters fight. After undergoing a rigorous hour of calisthenics, judo holds and flips, the students welcomed a 10-minute break.

At 2:00 pm, students marched to another classroom to learn about traffic control. The lectures were short and the class spent most of the period practicing hand signals. New troopers always thought that directing traffic was a simple matter accomplished by waving arms at cars past a corner. The one or two occasions that students tried it, however, demonstrated that if the cars were moving faster than ox carts, it took a bit of practice to make the right signal at the right time. The classroom practice was a

Unarmed defense demonstration

substitute for practical work with actual traffic, which took place in a "traffic maze" behind the school buildings during the months before the snow came.

In the next class the student might attend a lecture on the organization of the Constabulary. Students were always interested in learning about how their squadrons and outposts fit into the scheme for the occupation policing of the American Zone. Large-scale situation maps displayed in the classroom presented this scheme most clearly. After class was over troopers marched back to the barracks to clean up for supper at 5:00 p.m.

Retreat formation was held at 5:45 for all classes when

Outdoor calisthenics. Mount Grünten 'Guard of the Allgäu' in background

daylight permitted. During the two mid-winter courses retreat formation was not held because of darkness, and mess call for supper was at 5:30. After mess, on all but two nights a week, the trooper was free to enjoy the movies, go to the service club, the enlisted men's club, the library, the gymnasium, one of the snack bars, the craft shop, the game room, or the Red Cross Club. There was a non-commissioned officers (NCO) club in the center of town, and enlisted men's and student officer's clubs on the school site.

Each day special services trucks were dispatched to Munich to procure beer and supplies for the various clubs. Liquor supplies obtained from Antwerp were rationed (two ounces per week) for all enlisted personnel. Movies, also obtained from Munich, were shown for two nights and then returned. The Red Cross also put on several live shows performed by both the Red Cross hostesses and by various traveling German entertainers.

Church services for Catholics and Protestants were held daily and special services were held on Sundays.

On Tuesday and Thursday nights the platoons were assembled in their homerooms and given a two-hour written exam. Questions were given and text references assigned from which the trooper could find the required information.

Following the day's classroom work, the trooper usually returned to his quarters to review his notes, write letters or just relax prior to lights out and taps at 11:00 pm.

Upon the completion of all courses, the students were given two ratings: an academic rating and a disciplinary rating. The academic rating was the average of all the graded tests taken; the disciplinary rating was based on the student's conduct

Student
examinations

while attending the school, and was designated excellent, very satisfactory, satisfactory, or unsatisfactory. Students who attained excellent disciplinary ratings and the highest academic ratings in their platoons were designated honor students and received recognition at graduation ceremonies.

CHAPTER TWELVE

THE CONSTABULARY BECOMES OPERATIONAL

Perhaps then-Lieutenant Colonel A. F. Irzyk, Chief of Staff at Constabulary Headquarters, said it best when he wrote, "Very quietly and unobtrusively a new force took control of the policing of the United States Zone of Occupation in Germany..."[1] Without a parade, ceremony, or any fanfare, the United States Constabulary became operational—assuming all responsibilities for carrying out the objectives of the U.S. government in the U.S. Zone of occupation—on July 1, 1946.

According to Gen. Harmon as reflected in his memoirs of the earliest days of the Constabulary[2], the operational plan was to divide the American Zone into three areas, each to be controlled by one of the three brigades. Each brigade area was then divided into three regimental areas, which in turn were divided into three battalion areas (ultimately 27 battalion areas) and so on to the company and platoon level.

"We had excellent communications, the very best that the American Expeditionary Force (AEF) afforded in radio, telegraph, and telephone.

"In order to develop an esprit de corps we had the colors of blue and yellow on our helmets and on all the vehicles. We had a special Constabulary patch, which I personally designed, made up of the colors of the infantry, cavalry, and artillery, with a red blitz going down through them. These three branches of the Army furnished the majority of our troops. We never did get to the figure of 35,000. I believe 32,000 was our maximum strength.

"To enable me to get around and inspect my troops I had a private train. This train was one of the four trains used by Hitler and his staff. My train had been used by Hermann Goering. It had three cars with a diesel engine in each of the end cars. One car was set up as a dining room and kitchen. The middle car was for sleeping quarters for the staff, and the last car was a lounge car with radio and a regular conference car. This train had the right-of-way over all the tracks in Bavaria and went speeding through the countryside. Some days I was able to inspect three and four battalions in one day.

"I made it a point to inspect each one of the 27 battalions at least once a month, which meant almost one battalion per day as an average. Also, that I was on the road practically all of the time.

"I would take my operations staff with me on these inspections and cover the shortages in supply, inspect the training, and look over the troops myself personally.

"We insisted on the highest type of military courtesy and discipline, also in personal appearance. The men became quite proud of themselves and soon became the outstanding soldiers in the AEF. To develop an organization like this was sort of unpopular with what was going on in the rest of the AEF at the time.

"The Stars and Stripes, the AEF soldier paper, had a column known as the 'B Bag' in which the enlisted men could criticize their officers and complain about the discipline.

"One of the first things I did was to announce to my command that there would be no Constabulary soldier writing for the B Bag. If they had anything they wanted to complain about they would complain in the regular manner as prescribed in Army regulations. They could always come to see me, the Commander of the Constabulary. I would assure that they got a fair hearing, but there would be no one that could write to the B Bag and remain in the Constabulary."

One soldier attempted to write to the B Bag. But Harmon got wind of it, held a parade formation, stripped the man of his Constabulary insignia, and had him transferred out of his regiment.

"The newspaper reporters, having heard me talk about the B Bag, went to General McNarney [Commander of US. Forces, European Theater] about it, and said that something ought to be done, that I was curbing freedom of speech.

"General McNarney said, 'Well, General Harmon will take care of himself,' and said nothing about it to me. I think he was probably secretly pleased, like most all of the officers were, that somebody was having a little discipline the way the old Army used to have it.

"The Stars and Stripes, as I saw it after the war, was one of the worst influences against good discipline and order of anything that happened in the AEF.

"We were having a lot of trouble with the colored soldier; although he formed only 10% of the actual manpower, he was committing 90% of the crimes, which consisted mostly of stealing rations and sex crimes and fighting among themselves.

"We had one particular battalion in the southern sector. I sent one Constabulary trooper down there and told him that the first time anybody spoke out of turn to shoot him right between the eyes, that I would protect him. I wanted these people to realize that when one Constabulary trooper came down to see that the law was obeyed, like the Canadian Mounted Police, he had the whole Constabulary behind him.

"He went down there alone and soon was required to shoot a colored soldier in the line of duty. We immediately court-martialed him, cleared him, and had no more trouble with that battalion. In fact, the soldier got along fine with the battalion; it was just a bad element that was giving us trouble anyway.

"To develop a fine organization like this it was imperative that I have topflight leaders. I ended up with what I believed were nine of the finest colonels that we could find. They were really good. Also the battalion commanders on down to the company officers at least were equally good.

"I remember one battalion commander complaining to me that one of his regimental commanders didn't know much and was very poor in administration. He had done well as a combat leader at the front during the war and had risen from a platoon commander to a battalion commander. I told the colonel that if he was good enough to advance like that it was up to the colonel to train him in his paperwork and administration and that if he couldn't do it I would get some colonel that could. That closed that issue, and the man soon developed into a very fine leader in a more or less peace-time situation that we were confronted with."

Harmon's memoir continued:[3]

"As stated before, our greatest problem in Germany was our own soldiers. We had practically no problem with the German people. They were used to giving respect and obedience to the Army. They used to come around and watch our inspections, and we put on quite a little bit of a show purposely for their benefit.

"Most of the trouble, outside of the colored problem just referred to, was the speeding up and down the roads of the soldiers in the AEF, with the result of tremendous high casualties in deaths in automobile accidents. As I recall it, we had around 150 a week at one time.

"To rectify this we set up speed traps throughout the zone with court-martial power to handle the cases right on the spot. After about two weeks of the operation of these speed traps with a prompt trial and sentencing of soldiers and officers, we cut the death rate to about one-third in a very short time. I have often thought it was too bad that we couldn't do this in civil life. People wouldn't stand it. They would have all kinds of lawyers to quibble with the law. We dealt justly and doled it out on the spot. We even caught General Eisenhower one time, who was cruising around with his driver at 90 miles an hour."

Less than six months after it became operational, Constabulary work was at its peak. Over 146,000 roadblocks had been set and 6,200 speed traps had been established. Reconnaissance planes

Constabulary speed trap on the Autobahn

logged over 15,000 hours in air missions, and check-and-search operations resulted in over 1,350 arrests. More importantly, border patrols were intensified with over 80,000 patrols by horse-mounted platoons, foot soldiers, and motorcycles and other vehicles, resulting in a dramatic decrease in black market operations, smuggling, and traffic accidents.

THE WOMEN'S ARMY CORP ARRIVES IN SONTHOFEN

The first contingent of the Women's Army Corp (WACs) arrived in Sonthofen in September of 1946 just as classes at the school were at their peak. The rapid turnover in personnel caused by redeployment created an urgent need for replacements. The group of women included four officers and sixty enlisted personnel, most of whom were assigned to the Constabulary School Squadron and to the various sections of the Headquarters and Academic Division where shortages were most critical.

YOUTH PROGRAMS

The Office of Military Government initiated new Youth Activity Programs throughout the occupation zone to assist in the organization and activities of youth groups. In August 1946, speaking at a conference on youth problems, Gen. Joseph T. McNarney, European Theater commander, said:

"I think what we hope to achieve is that a greater number of German youth will absorb our democratic ideals, and that they in turn will become the future leaders of the German nation which they will be in a relatively short time, and that they will lead the German nation along the path of democracy so that it will not be necessary for us to again come to Europe to wage war."

Officers and non-commissioned officers were assigned to

actively participate in assisting German Youth Committees. School principals also assisted. Athletic programs and sports clinics were organized, Army surplus sports equipment became available, and youth centers became operational in many of the largest cities and towns.

DISPLACED PERSONS

Another problem faced by the Constabulary was the maintaining of law and order among displaced persons. By the summer of 1946 some 365,000 people in the American Zone were displaced. They could not—for various reasons, including political fears among the displaced—be repatriated to their homelands. This population was made up largely of Jews, Poles, Estonians, Lithuanians, and Latvians, most of whom had fled before the advancing Soviet Army, preferring internment in Germany rather than a life in their own Soviet-dominated homelands.

Arguably, the most daunting problem the Constabulary dealt with regarding the displaced-person population was the number of incidents that took place involving black market activities, robbery, larceny, and civil disorder. Such incidents were usually motivated by a desire to obtain food, money, and other essentials. But it nevertheless proved to be a challenge for Constabulary troops who were constantly called on to maintain surveillance and exert control over displaced-persons camps. This challenge remained until the United Nations Relief and Rehabilitation Administration began its programs of reparation and resettlement.

Harmon would write[4]:

"The biggest problem to me was the displaced persons. ...The most difficult were the Jewish people. They were guilty of most of the black market offenses and were the special pets of the Democratic administration at home. No matter how much we tried to treat them fairly and at the same time make them behave, we were always subject to criticism by committees who came over from the States. These committees were chiefly made up of Jewish people who were very quick to criticize and resent any disciplinary action we took to keep these people behaving as they should and curb their black market activities.

"The next most difficult people were the Poles. They were a type of people that would break out and have lots of fights among themselves and among the German people. We found them very hot-tempered and difficult to handle. They were black marketers like the people in the Jewish camps.

"The Jewish camps were always inclined to be dirty and they presented a constant problem to have them kept clean and in a sanitary condition. The Poles were not much better.

"The finest people we had to handle were the Baltic people—the Lithuanians, Estonians, and Latvians. They were neat and clean. They kept their camps neat and busied themselves making articles that they could sell made by their own hands, everything legitimate. They were very fine people. Indeed, I wish we had more of them in our own country. It was a pleasure to have these people.

"All told, we had several million of these displaced people to take care of pending their transfer to their homeland, or in the case of the Jews, to be shipped south to Palestine. With all the training problems and the problems of the German people and of our own Army, and the problems created by the displaced persons, we still had another. In the provinces of Sacony and Turengia we faced the Russian Army.

"I had had experience facing the Russian Army in Czechoslovakia and that experience was very useful to me now in facing the 8th Russian Guards Army under General Proznik in Germany.

"Shortly after taking over the operational duties of the Constabulary I made an appointment to visit him inside the Russian lines. We had a very friendly meeting, everything being passed through interpreters. I was successful in getting his cooperation in the establishing of ports of entry like we had had in Czechoslovakia, and also we established a clearer line of demarcation between my front and his by the building of watchtowers every five to ten miles.

"At our dinner that noon what interested me most was that all during the conference there was a commissar from Moscow who did most of the talking. He had graduated from CCNY in the United States and was fully conversant with the English language.

"During dinner I had a big Cossack general on my right and General Proznik was on my left. Neither one apparently could say a word of English. Suddenly the commissar was ordered away in answer to a telephone call. As soon as he left the big Cossack on my right turned to me and said in perfect English, 'Now that that son-of-a-bitch is gone you and I can talk.' General Proznik immediately talked excellent English. I found that he was a connoisseur of snakes. He was born in the Caucasus and knew more about poisonous snakes in my own country than I did myself. We had a very jolly, happy meeting from then on. Everybody joked and laughed and we really had a wonderful time with our Russian Army friends now that the commissar was out of the question."

Harmon added that the members of the Russian Army were afraid of the NKVD, the notorious Soviet secret police and predecessor to the infamous KGB.

"Apparently they had members of this organization throughout every echelon of command who were superior in giving orders to the Army commander with whom they served. It made it very difficult for the Army to do anything without referring to these commissars, especially when any question of relations with the American Army was concerned."

CHAPTER THIRTEEN

HARMON BIDS FAREWELL

On May 1, 1947, Gen. Harmon turned over command to Maj. Gen. Withers Burress.

Harmon's farewell message follows[1]:

"The Constabulary was created as an instrument to help win the peace. It has as its primary mission the security of the U.S. Zone of Germany, the support of Military Government policies and assistance to law enforcement agencies in the restoration and maintenance of order. As a result of insistence on high standards of discipline, personal appearance and duty, the Constabulary has developed itself into a fine organization, which is today a distinct credit to the United States, to the Occupation Force and to the individual officer and enlisted man who fill its ranks. The Constabulary has also had a far-reaching effect and influence in raising the general behavior and appearance of all personnel in the Zone. It has established itself in the confidence of the German people as a just organization which is striving to assist them in restoring normal conditions of life.

"As a soldier who took part in the first phase of the war, which required the destruction of the German army, I am very happy to have had the opportunity to command the Constabulary and direct its development in the second phase, the winning of the peace. This opportunity for service is sufficient reward for me for any effort I have expended, and I will always look upon it as one of the periods of my career when I was able to give something in a real constructive way. In leaving the Constabulary I only hope that the individual integrity of the officer and trooper will be continually stressed and that duty will always be performed with justice. By so doing we can assure the Constabulary a deserved honorable mention when the history of this war is written.

"I am deeply grateful to all the officers and men of the Constabulary who have worked so conscientiously to develop the present efficiency, morale and high standards. I know you will continue your efforts under the new Commander. My best wishes go to all of you for the future."

Harmon would later write:

"I packed up my goods and prepared to leave for the United States. We were to sail from Bremerhaven, Germany.

It was arranged that my Constabulary train would move me, my family, and baggage from Heidelberg to Bremerhaven, leaving Heidelberg at 7:30 in the morning.

"As my car drove through the streets of Heidelberg to the station I was surprised to see the sidewalks lined with German people at that early hour, who had come voluntarily to see me go away and gave me a big hand as my automobile passed along the street. This action really cheered me and made me realize that the Constabulary had won its place in the respect and approval of the German people.

"They knew that we had tried to bring justice and order to the countryside, to treat everyone fairly, to curb crime, black market and unfavorable and unfair conditions. I always will appreciate this voluntary turnout and this silent tribute to me by the German people, at 7:30 in the morning, in Heidelberg!"

Harmon arrived at Bremerhaven and boarded ship. As the vessel weighed anchor and eased out of the harbor, he recalled standing on the stern and watching the German coastline disappear:

"I began to think about going home and realized as never before what a wonderful country we had in America, where men were free to go from one town to another, from one state to another, without police stopping them, or having visas to go from one part of the country to the other without being stopped for passports and inspection.

"The people of the United States have no idea of the great freedom they enjoy and the high standard of living, the wonderful stores with all kinds of groceries, dry goods, etc. that they have the privilege of going to and shopping in.

"We have never been invaded since the Revolutionary war [the general obviously forgetting the War of 1812]. We don't know what it is to be driven from our homes and leave them burning and to carry all of our possessions that we have in a little cart or in a bag slung over our shoulders. Sometimes I think it would be a good thing if our people could go through one tough experience like these people have to that are in a land devastated by war. They would then be more appreciative of their country and we would hear less and see less about draft dodgers, speeches against our wonderful land with its great opportunities and high standard of living that everyone can enjoy who is willing to work."

CHAPTER FOURTEEN
THE CONSTABULARY MISSION CHANGES

Shortly after Harmon's departure, the mission of the U.S. Constabulary changed, and understandably so.

Almost from the beginning of the Allied occupation, the Soviet Union had begun a systematic transformation of its vast sector, from an occupied zone to a military stronghold. And the Allies became concerned over the buildup of large armored forces along the Russian-American border.

Various incidents related to the Soviet buildup increased at an alarming rate, thus compelling the Constabulary to institute strict border-control procedures. Inter-zonal travel became difficult, necessitating a substantial increase of Constabulary troops assigned to border patrolling. The troops were supplemented by air patrols, M8 armored car patrols and horse patrols to cover terrain not accessible by vehicles. Russian border crossing points were relocated and strengthened. New sentry posts were established, patrols were increased on the border, and air reconnaissance was instituted on a continuing schedule.

As the beginning of the Cold War began to reveal itself, the threat of Soviet forces triggered a change in policy, and in early 1947 there was a major reorganization of Constabulary forces. Gone were the raids, speed traps, and roadblocks. Constabulary commands instituted new tactical training programs, and the Constabulary quickly evolved into a combat-ready military force. The Office of Military Government U.S. Zone assumed responsibility for border control from the Constabulary, and turned most of it over to the newly rearmed German Land Border Police.

There were many reasons for the diminishing role of the Constabulary as a military police force. The German population showed no animosity toward the occupation forces, no civil disorders materialized, and the German police were trained to assume more responsibilities for internal security, patrolling and policing functions. However, the Constabulary did continue to man border crossing points for members of the occupation force not subject to German police jurisdiction.

Soon thereafter, the Department of the Army deactivated the Constabulary School Squadron and most of the teaching staff. As departments began to shut down, school personnel were reassigned almost on a daily basis to new units throughout the occupation zone in preparation for response to the Russian threat. Although the school continued to operate on a limited basis, courses taught were in non-Constabulary subjects.

TRANSFER TO G-2

On July 2, 1947, I received a letter from Lt. Col. Archibald

Eaton, our department director, in which I learned that I was being transferred to the G-2 Intelligence Section, and would remain in Sonthofen. The department was under the command of Lt. Col. John P. Stone.

Because the Constabulary units were spread throughout the occupation zone, they were in a better position to gather intelligence and evaluate it. The emphasis on intelligence collection and liaison with other agencies—Counterintelligence Corps (CIC), Criminal Investigation Division (CID), Military Government and German police—became of paramount importance.[1] Classes were held weekly to impress upon the troops the importance of intelligence collection. Thus the Constabulary was able to remain informed of any activities in the zone which might threaten internal security.

My immediate responsibilities were to read and evaluate reports submitted to our section by Constabulary outposts as well as other agencies with whom we had established liaisons. The reports primarily dealt with black market activities and illegal border crossings.

Of particular interest to G-2 was the filtering down through Bavaria of Nazi war criminals and SS men attempting to leave Germany. We learned through various sources and informants that the escape route out of Germany was through Memmingen in the Allgaü's secluded wooded regions near the Austrian and Swiss borders to Lake Constance, the Brenner Pass or on to Switzerland. From there, they would make their way to Italy, where the International Red Cross helped relocate refugees to their native lands or to South America. After all information was evaluated, military units and agencies were alerted in those areas where the infiltrations were reported to be.

Two months later, it all changed for me.

INFORMATION AND EDUCATION SCHOOL IN HEIDELBERG

Lt. Col. Stone called me into his office and explained that under the new Army initiative, all enlisted troops would be receiving a minimum of one hour per week instruction on world events. And, under his direction, I was to be the Non-Commissioned Officer (NCO) administering the new Information and Education (I&E) program for all school personnel. The following day, I received orders to report to the University of Heidelberg for two weeks of training in the methods of teaching and disseminating information.

It was indeed a thrill to be studying at the University of Heidelberg. The buildings were impressive, as was the university's history. In addition to attending classes, I met many new friends, cruised up and down the Rhine, and enjoyed a lot of sightseeing.

Two weeks later, I was back at Sonthofen, where each week I received an Army informational newsletter and subjects for discussion for that week. One of the subjects was our relationship with our Allies. I had a hell of a hard time convincing my classes that the Russians were our friends, particularly since the Constabulary was transforming itself to meet any potential Soviet military threat.

My I&E assignment not only enabled me to keep abreast of world events, but also afforded me the opportunity to fish, swim, boat, and continue my skiing at the Army ski school at Garmisch.

In October, I received word that my grandmother was gravely ill and I was granted an emergency furlough to visit her. I shipped out of Bremerhaven and arrived just before she passed away. One week later, I received my orders to report to Fort Benning, Georgia. While serving there I learned that in March of 1948, five months after my return to the states, Gen. Lucius D. Clay, commander-in-chief of the European command, announced that the school would close effective July 1.

In May 1948, Maj. Gen. I. D. White assumed command of the Constabulary from Maj. Gen. Louis Craig. Gen. White transitioned the Constabulary from a police force into a highly mobile, hard-hitting armored command. It became one of the two primary combat forces in the European Theater and the largest armored force in the Army at that time.

In the fall of 1950, President Harry S. Truman announced a buildup of American forces in Europe to meet American commitments in the new NATO alliance. As a result, the U.S. Seventh Army was re-activated on Nov. 24, replacing Constabulary headquarters.

The 1st Infantry Division and the Constabulary units were assigned to the Seventh Army. The 1st Constabulary Brigade was deactivated on Aug. 15, 1951, followed by the deactivation of the 2nd Constabulary Brigade on Nov. 15. Although the Seventh Army and its tactical units had been made responsible for the security of the Eastern borders, the 15th and 24th Constabulary Squadrons remained to carry out the peacetime border security mission.

With the arrival of the 4th Infantry Division and the assumption of border security by the 15th ACR of V Corps in 1952, the 15th and 24th Constabulary Squadrons were deactivated in December.

The Constabulary had a short history compared with other units of the Army. But despite its brief history, the Constabulary was unmatched in its "esprit de corps," record of achievement, and overall service to country and to Germany.

The Constabulary soldier with his distinctive uniform and gold-and-blue striped vehicles was a formidable sight in every section of the American Zone. The badge of the Constabulary— the lightning bolt brilliantly displayed on a field of blue and gold—and the motto "Mobility, Vigilance, Justice!" reflected the efficiency of American occupation-force soldiers, who have often been credited with laying the foundation of democracy in Germany.

TODAY U.S. CONSTABULARY SOLDIERS OF WORLD WAR II ARE THE FORGOTTEN PEACEKEEPERS.

But perhaps with American forces deployed worldwide— tasked with all manner of duties from conventional war fighting and special operations (including counterinsurgencies) to peacekeeping and occupation (and with each duty often overlapping in an asymmetrical environment)—the U.S. Constabulary's existence and performance may provide lessons for how best to organize, train, equip, and deploy occupation forces in the 21st century.

After all, what better foundation might there be for modern ground forces than that they be designed for high "mobility," ever "vigilant," and—working closely with civilian communities on foreign shores—imbued with a sense of "justice."

As General Harmon said in his farewell speech[2] before leaving for the U.S., "I hope that the individual integrity of the officers and troopers will be continually stressed and the duty will always be performed with justice. By so doing we can assure the Constabulary a deserved honorable mention when the history of this war is written."

NOTES

Introduction

1. Byrnes Speech of Hope. Delivered by U.S. Secretary of State James F. Byrnes, September 6, 1946.

Chapter 1

1. Hartmut Happel. History of the Ordensburg Sonthofen. (Immenstadt: J. Eberl KG, 2003), 10.

(Captain Harmut Happel is a member of the General Staff at the former Ordensburg, which is today called the General Oberest Beck-Kaserne, home to the Feldjäger Military Police School of the German Federal Armed Forces, Headquarters Service School, and the Bundswehr Sportschule Training Center.)

Chapter 2

1. United States Army Military History Institute, Carlisle Barracks, Pennsylvania. Colonel Henry C. Newton Papers.

Chapter 3

1. German-American Fellowship of MN, and Catholic Encylopedia Vol. XIV. Robert Appleton Company: 1912.

2. Publishing House, National Socialist Democratic Workers Party, Munich, 1937.

Chapter 4

1. Die Adolf Hitler Schule 1941. Translation by Gerhard Kirchner, Certified Interpreter, August 6, 1946.

Chapter 5

1. United States Army Military History Institute, Carlisle Barracks, Pennsylvania. Colonel Henry C. Newton Papers.

Chapter 10

1. The Battle of Stalingrad. http://www.historylearningsite.co.uk/battle_of_stalingrad.html (accessed January 15, 2008).

Chapter 12

1. Lieutenant Colonel A. F. Irzyk, Cavalry. "'Mobility, Vigilance, Justice': A Saga of the Constabulary." Military Review, March 1947. http://www.geocities.com/usconstabulary/MilRev.Mar1947.html (accessed May 28, 2001).

2. E. N. Harmon, et al. Combat Commander: Autobiography of a Soldier. (Englewood, NJ: Prentice Hall, 1970), 180. Courtesy of Norwich University, Special Collections Krietzberg Library, Northfield, Vermont.

3. Ibid., 181-182.

4. Ibid., 182.

Chapter 13

1. E. N. Harmon, et al. Combat Commander: Autobiography of a Soldier. (Englewood, NJ: Prentice Hall, 1970), 183-184.

Chapter 14

1. H. P. Rand, Captain, Field Artillery. "A Progress Report on the United States Constabulary." Military Review, October 1949. http:// www.14th-acr.org/history48.html (accessed July 11, 2001).

2. E. N. Harmon, Major General, G. S. C., Commanding. "General Harmon Bids Farewell in Message to Constabulary." The Lightning Bolt, May 1, 1947.

REFERENCES

Bess, Demaree. "How We Botched the Occupation in Germany." *Saturday Evening Post*, January 26, 1946.

Die Adolf Hitler Schule 1941. Kempten, Germany: Allgaüer Drucherel Und Verlageanftalt National Socialist Democratic Workers Party, 1941.

Happel, Harmut. *History of the Ordensburg Sonthofen*. Immenstadt, Germany: J. Eberl KG, 2003.

Harmon, Ernest N., Milton MacKaye, William Ross MacKaye. *Combat Commander: Autobiography of a Soldier*. Englewood, NJ: Prentice Hall, 1970.

History of the U.S. Constabulary 10 January 1946—31 December 1946. Historical Division Headquarters European Command APO 757, Germany: European Command Historical Division, 1947.

Irzyk, Alvin F. "'Mobility, Vigilance, Justice': A Saga of the Constabulary." *Military Review* 26 (March 1947): 13-21.

Kaufman, D. A. "The U.S. Constabulary Forces in Germany 1946-52." *Trading Post*. Worth, IL: July-September, 1993.

Rand, H. P. "A Progress Report on the United States Constabulary." *Military Review* (October 1949).

Rutledge, L. A. "The Twilight Cavalry Men." *America's Military Heritage 1* (Summer 1992): 6-16.

Snyder, James M. *The Establishment and Operations of the United States Constabulary 3 October 1945—30 June 1947*. Historical sub-section C-3, Washington, D.C.: GPO 1947.

Sondern, F., Jr. "The United States Constabulary: A New Force in Germany." *Reader's Digest*, 1947.

Stacy, William E. "U.S. Army Border Operations in Germany 1945-1983." Headquarters U.S. Army, Europe and 7th Army: Military History Office, GSM 5-1-84.

U.S. Army Center of Military History, "The U.S. Constabulary in post-war Germany 1946-52." DAMH-FPO: April, 2000, updated February 2009.

PHOTO CREDITS

1. General Ernest N. Harmon, Commanding General, United States Constabulary.

2. The 'Ordensburg': former Hitler Youth School, served as U.S. Constabulary School 1946-1948. Courtesy of John Medak.

2A. The Constabulary Insignia designed by General Harmon. Courtesty of John Capone.

2B. Mount Grünten 'Guard of the Allgaü'. Courtesy John Capone.

3. Dr. Robert Ley, Leader, National Socialist Democratic Workers Party (NDSAP).

3A. German workers marching in support of Hitler Deutschland Erwacht 1933.

4. Construction of road from Ordensburg to Town of Sonthofen. Heimhuber Photo, Courtesy of Hartmut Happel.

4A. Celebration of Completion of First Phase of Construction. Heimhuber Photo, Courtesy of Hartmut Happel

5. Dedication of the Bell Tower. Courtesy of Heimhuber fotohaus.

5A. Ordensburg Marienburg in Malbork, Poland.

6. Teutonic Knights during the Third Crusade.

6A. Cross of the Teutonic Order.

6B. Dr. Robert Ley at the Hitler Youth School; to his right, Architect Hermann Geisler and School Commandant Bauer. Heimhuber Photo, Courtesy of Hartmut Happel.

6C. Hitler Youth School students. Courtesty of Die Hitler Youth Schule.

7. Hitler Youth Student Body School Formation. Courtesy of Die Hitler Youth Schule.

8. Dr. Ley reviewing student application. Heimhuber Photo, Courtesy of Hartmut Happel.

8A. Applicant before student review board. Courtesty of Die Hitler Youth Schule.

9. Room inspection at the Hitler Youth School. Courtesy of Die Hitler Youth Schule.

10. Hitler Youth School students marching through Sonthofen. Courtesy of Die Hitler Youth Schule.

11. Sonthofen church and retirement home bombed during 1945 air raid. Heimhuber Photo, Courtesy of Hartmut Happel.

12. Communications class at the Constabulary School. Heimhuber Photo, Courtesy of Hartmut Happel.

13. General Harmon inspecting 6th Constabulary Squadron vehicles. Courtesy of Ralph Stovall.

13A. General Harmon inspecting Headquarters Troop and Medical Detachment 6th Squadron. Courtesy of Ralph Stovall.

14. Colonel Henry C. Newton, Assistant Commandant, U.S. Constabulary School. Heimhuber Photo, Courtesy of Hartmut Happel.

15. Colonel Newton conducts inspection of Constabulary School department heads. Heimhuber Photo, Courtesy of Hartmut Happel.

16. Special 3-day orientation course briefing for Field Grade Officers. Heimhuber Photo, Courtesy of Hartmut Happel.

17. Orientation for new student body. Heimhuber Photo, Courtesy of Hartmut Happel.

18. Students listen to welcoming address by School Commandant. Heimhuber Photo, Courtesy of Hartmut Happel.

19A. Unarmed defense class. Courtesy of John Capone.

20. Constabulary School graduation. Courtesy of John Medak.

21. Classroom Instruction. Heimhuber Photo, Courtesy of Hartmut Happel.

22. Student Officer Corps. Heimhuber Photo, Courtesy of Hartmut Happel.

23. European Armed Forces staff officers School Graduation. Heimhuber Photo, Courtesy of Hartmut Happel.

24. U.S. Constabulary School Commandant, Colonel John J. Binns. Heimhuber Photo, Courtesy of Hartmut Happel

24A. Student formation. Heimhuber Photo, Courtesy of Hartmut Happel.

25. Dining Hall. Heimhuber Photo, Courtesy of Hartmut Happel.

26. Marching to classrooms. Courtesy of John Capone.

27. Classroom Instruction. Heimhuber Photo, Courtesy of Hartmut Happel.

28. Classroom Instruction. Heimhuber Photo, Courtesy of Hartmut Happel.

29. Unarmed defense demonstration. Courtesy of John Capone.

29A. Student Judo Demonstration by S/Sgt. John Capone and S/Sgt. Frank Broce. Courtesy of John Capone.

30. Outdoor calisthenics. Courtesy of John Capone.

31. Student examinations. Heimhuber Photo, Courtesy of Hartmut Happel.

32. Constabulary Speed trap on the Autobahn.

John Capone's book 'Forgotten Peacekeepers' was inspired by his experience as a member of the teaching staff at the U.S. Constabulary School in Sonthofen, Germany from March, 1946 to October, 1947. A member of Special Troops, he participated in the training and preparation of these highly dedicated police-soldiers serving a major role in the peacekeeping mission. John Capone and his wife Diana Ballard live in Pompano Beach, Florida. John is a retired real estate developer, and graduate and past Alumni President of Southern Connecticut State University. This is his first book.

www.ingramcontent.com/pod-product-compliance
Lightning Source LLC
Chambersburg PA
CBHW060351090426
42734CB00011B/2109